Basic Writing

Other Prentice Hall Regents books by Joy M. Reid:

The Process of Paragraph Writing
The Process of Composition
Teaching ESL Writing

Basic Writing

Second Edition

Joy M. Reid
University of Wyoming

Illustrations by E. Shelley Reid

Prentice Hall Regents

Library of Congress Cataloging-in-Publication Data

Reid, Joy M.
    Basic Writing / Joy M. Reid : illustrations by E. Shelley Reid.
  2nd ed.

      p.   cm.
   ISBN 0-13-353657-2
   1. English language—Rhetoric—Problems, exercises, etc.
  2. English language—Textbooks for foreign speakers.   I. Reid
Shelley. II. Title.
PE1413.R36   1996   95–46972
428.2'4—dc20   CIP

Editor: *Sheryl Olinsky*
Publisher: *Mary Jane Peluso*
Director of Production and Manufacturing: *Aliza Greenblatt*
Editorial Production/Design Manager: *Dominick Mosco*
Cover Design: *Warren Fischbach*
Art Director: *Merle Krumper*
Manufacturing Manager: *Ray Keating*

Printed in the United States of America

10   9   8   7   6

ISBN 0-13-353657-2

Contents

Preface   *xi*

1   Family   *1*

2 Home 27

3 Country 55

4   Culture   *87*

5   Travel Experiences   *113*

6   First Impressions, First Problems   *141*

7   Adjustments and Solutions   *171*

8   Similarities and Differences   *199*

Appendices

Preface

Basic Writing (BW) is a textbook for ESL students whose English language proficiency is limited. These students are not beginners; rather they form a broad group of "false beginners," students with limited English language skills whose overall proficiency is more advanced than their English writing skills. The assumptions I have made about these students are that they already know something about, and are capable of learning more about the following

- basic paragraph structure (a series of sentences about one idea)
- a sense of linear sequencing
- some English vocabulary about shared experiences
- how to select and use appropriate connectors
- grammar structures commonly used in writing;
- combining sentences

Rationale

It is unreasonable to expect students who are inexperienced in both the language and processes of written U.S. prose to "pick a topic and write a paragraph." One pedagogical approach that meets the needs of these ESL students is to consider recent ESL and native English speaker (NES) theoretical and classroom research in composing. Accordingly, I developed the organization of the materials in the first edition of BW in light of four areas of research: schema theory, communicative competence, learning styles, and classroom community.*

Organization

In *Basic Writing,* the chapters are arranged thematically, with three to six paragraphs about single topics (e.g., "My Family," "A Holiday in My Country") that describe common student experiences. The paragraphs follow the general rhetorical form of U.S. academic

---

* For a fuller discussion of these research areas, see the Teacher's Manual for *Basic Writing.* I write textbooks for students, and teacher's manuals for teachers. The Teacher's Manual for *Basic Writing* contains suggestions for teaching, approaches for helping students investigate their styles and strategies, and an annotated bibliography for further reading. It also contains sample syllabi, activities for teaching paragraph revision, and more student sample paragraphs for teaching and testing. For a free copy of the Teacher's Manual, contact Prentice Hall Regents, Upper Saddle River, NJ, 07458.

prose, yet their content is directly relevant and available to the student readers. In other words, the paragraph topics tap the prior experiences of the readers ("Preparing for a Trip," "My Country's Flag") and present their opinions ("What Surprised Me about the United States," "What I Miss about My Country"). Moreover, reading the paragraphs gives the students basic vocabulary, general background information, and grammatical structures for their own paragraphs.

In addition to the thematically organized chapters, nontext materials in BW reflect concepts and skills pertinent to U.S. academic prose. Line drawings, photographs, charts, and maps, as well as surveys and questionnaires, emerge from the themes of the chapters. These materials are designed to appeal to, and to provide practice for, the students in preacademic writing tasks: explaining, describing, discussing, and analyzing. They encourage the students to solve problems, seek advice, and draw conclusions.

Objectives

First, effective writing occurs when writers understand the writing context and are able to fulfill the expectations of their readers. ESL students are often unsuccessful writers because they do not understand the context in which they are trying to communicate. Therefore, one of the purposes of BW is to prepare students for the rhetorical expectations of the academic audience. However, that purpose is presented implicitly rather than explicitly; such conventions as the topic sentence are not explained directly. Instead, students are encouraged, through continuous writing, peer review, and teacher intervention, to discover the conventions of academic prose format.

Second, the material in BW provides students with opportunities to strengthen their English language skills. The authentic paragraphs in BW present student writers with a variety of incremental language challenges inductively, in such areas as vocabulary, grammar, and sentence structures that are <u>displayed</u>—but not explained in detail—throughout the book. Students begin by practicing simpler structures and vocabulary, gradually increasing their linguistic schema. Furthermore, numerous exercises are contextualized within these student paragraphs, giving basic writers ample opportunity to recognize and/or produce the displayed language, ideas, and/or structures. Finally, paragraphs written by NESs, which are often more sophisticated in all of these areas, provide an additional challenge for student readers and writers.

Third, BW has a strong cultural component that has as its goal the communication of shared student experiences. Too often we think of international students as a rather homogeneous group. However, many basic writers are new to the language and the culture of U.S. academe; the limited language proficiency of those students often makes their initial problems in a post-secondary setting seem more isolated and severe. The paragraphs in BW give the student readers insights into that culture. Perhaps just as important, the students read about universal experiences that they can share: homesickness, culture shock, choosing a major, and adjustments to college/university life. For those studying in the U.S., the response to these paragraphs is often a relieved sigh of "me too"; the sharing of experiences in BW and in the "Interview" assignments allow the students to identify with their peers. In contrast, for students who are preparing to attend school in the U.S., the paragraphs in BW provide contexts, expectations, and perspectives that raise their awareness of, and enable them to better prepare for, their coming experiences.

Learning Styles

Because I have a particular interest in learning styles, I focused on that area as I wrote BW. Research in how ESL students learn best indicates that students learn in many different ways. Some prefer to learn visually, others aurally, still others kinesthetically (Reid, 1987). Students learn at different paces and in different rhythms; their strategies are influenced by "a wide range of factors, including aptitude, motivations, and cultural background" (Oxford-Carpenter, 1985). Some students are more analytic and field independent; others are more reflective and field dependent. Differences may exist among language backgrounds, educational backgrounds, and major fields. Some students learn more successfully by studying rules and gradually applying them; others prefer to immerse themselves and "risk" in learning situations. Given these variables, a writing textbook must allow for the wide scope of student interests, styles, and strategies (Reid, 1995).

In BW, the displayed grammar and sentence structures allow the "rule-learners" to recall the rule and apply it, while the "riskers" will probably brush through the displays, preferring, instead, to experiment. Moreover, the writing assignments permit different levels of response. Students who lack confidence may write more "controlled" paragraphs that are close to parts of one or more of the model paragraphs. As these students expand their vocabulary, identify a genuinely interesting topic, and feel more comfortable with writing, they will gradually branch out into more original work. More confident writers, and writers who prefer to take risks in their writing, will create more original paragraphs immediately.

Second Edition

For this edition of BW, I began with my students, asking them

- to identify their most and least favorite paragraphs

- to critique the grammar boxes

- to suggest improvements

- to analyze the problems they found, chapter by chapter

- to suggest solutions for those problems

I asked the reviewers for the same information, and, in addition, asked them specifically about my newest pedagogical interest, community building in the classroom. I also received feedback from teachers (and their students) who have used the first edition.

The results of that input, which I incorporated into this edition, are as follows:

- new student paragraphs

- more peer and group work

- more directions for writing assignments that carry students through some peer review and revision processes

- some reorganization of the theme-based paragraphs

- more paragraphs by native English speakers

Conclusion

The most surprising lesson I learned while writing and class testing the manuscript for the first edition of BW was how much, not how little, interested students can accomplish. When I first began putting this book together, I tended to underestimate the students, despite the fact that I had been teaching ESL and basic students for twenty years. My experiences with these students have shown me that the materials I have used for many years—primarily grammar-based texts that focused on sentence-level writing—while comfortable for the students, did not sufficiently motivate or challenge them. My basic writers, given interesting topics, encouraged to read and discuss the paragraphs of students who came before them (and succeeded), and provided opportunities to communicate directly with a variety of audiences, have produced enormous quantities of high quality written material. And so I wrote BW, with my students in mind, to provide challenges, high interest, and success for those students.

References

OXFORD-CARPENTER, R. (1985). Second-language learning strategies: what the research has to say. *ERIC/CLL News Bulletin* 9(1): 1–5.

REID, J. (1987). The learning style preferences of ESL students. *TESOL Quarterly* 20(3): 87-112.

REID, J., ed. (1995). *Using learning styles in the ESL/EFL classroom.* Heinle & Heinle.

Acknowledgments

My continued thanks to the initial reviewers of the first edition of BW, Ilona Leki (University of Tennessee) and Martha Pennington (City Polytechnic, Hong Kong); to teachers in the Intensive English Program at Colorado State University, especially Peggy Lindstrom, Eloise Ariza, and Jill Brand; to my students in the IEP, who gave me permission to use their paragraphs; and to my production manager at Prentice Hall, Dominic Mosco.

Many people also deserve thanks for their help with the second edition of *Basic Writing*. In particular, I appreciate the comments of the reviewers: Marianne Brems (Mission College, Santa Clara, CA); David Dahnke (North Harris College, Houston, TX); and Barbara Yanez (Devry Institute of Technology, Pomona, CA). I am also grateful for the comments of teachers using the text in the ELS Language Centers across the U.S.; of my basic writing students; and of my copyeditor at Prentice Hall Regents, Sylvia Moore.

My special thanks to my daughter, Shelley Reid, who re-drew several of the illustrations of BW (and who teaches ESL herself these days); to students and teachers I encountered while traveling in Hungary, Russia, and Ukraine, and whose writing now appears in BW; to my students, who willingly donated their writing and gave excellent feedback during the revision of the book; to the U.S. ESL teachers who generously communicated with me about their experiences abroad and their ESL basic writing experiences in the U.S.; and to Martha Hurst at the University of Wyoming, whose students provided informative paragraphs about U.S. cultures.

Finally, my thanks to Janet Constantinides, English Department Chair at the University of Wyoming, for her continued support; to Robert Hoskins, who worked tirelessly with me on the copyedited manuscript and the galleys for BW, and especially to my husband, Steve, whose shared composition knowledge, loving support, and sense of humor have inspired this book.

1
Family

MY FAMILY

My Mother

    I would like to write about the relationship between my mother and me. My mother is the person who has influenced me for more than twenty years. She is a beautiful woman, and she taught me principles of what is good and what is bad. She also told me about her religion. Now I am twenty years old, and I understand why she was strict with me. When I have a problem now, I call my mother because she is still the person who takes care of me.

Erich Backhoff
Mexico

TO BE

Present (now)			Past (yesterday)		
I	am		I	am	
he			he		
she	} is		she	} was	
it			it		
we			we		
you	} are		you	} were	
they			they		

My Family

My father WAS born in Honduras, and my mother IS from Mexico. There are eight children in my family, seven sons and me. I have two married brothers, and each brother has a daughter. My oldest brother IS a civil engineer, and my other brother IS an agronomy engineer. Also, I have two brothers studying in a technical college in Monterrey, Mexico. My two younger brothers ARE studying in high school in Honduras.

Maria Guadalupe Gabrie
Honduras

Exercise 1A

Write the TO BE verbs in the paragraph below.

My Sister and Brothers

My sister's name _____ Marta. She _____ twenty years old. She _____ married, and she has two daughters. She _____ a doctor, and she lives in Portugal. I have two brothers. Their names _____ Leonel and Alcino. They _____ thirty-two and twenty-four years old. Leonel lives in Keene, Texas. Alcino lives in Sao Tomé. They _____ married, but they do not have any children. Leonel _____ a businessman, and Alcino _____ a teacher.

Semoa de Sousa
Sao Tomé, West Africa

The Mother

The grass grows because of the spring sun,
but the grass can't give anything back to the sun in return.
It is the same with mother's love.
The love is so great and deep that a son, like inch-long grass,
can hardly return his mother's love.
How much love can the inch-long grass
give to the spring sun in return?

translated by
Prayat Laoprapossone
Thailand

TO HAVE

Present (now)		Past (yesterday)	
I	have	I	had
he she it	has	he she it	had
we you they	have	we you they	had

My Large Family

I HAVE a large family. They are in Venezuela. My family HAS ten people: my father, my mother, five sisters, two brothers, and me. My father HAS three brothers, and my mother HAS three sisters and one brother. All my uncles and my aunts live in Maracaibo City, but my family lives in Caracas. My father is 62 years old, and my mother is 54 years old. My father HAS a job at the Occidental Bank. He is a statistics supervisor. My mother doesn't work now, but she was a teacher and a director at the high school. I HAVE many cousins because my aunts and uncles are all married. My sisters are married too, and they HAVE many children. For example, my first sister is a doctor, and she HAS a child. My second sister is a dentist, and she HAS two children, one boy and one girl. My third sister is a doctor, and she HAS three children, two boys and one girl. My fourth and fifth sisters do not HAVE any children because they are not married.

José Ochea
Venezuela

Exercise 1B

Write the TO HAVE verbs in the paragraph below.

I

My Brother

My brother Evaristo is a special person in my life. He has helped me since I was born. He was always a good student and tried to be an example for my brothers and me. He was always number one in all sports, and for that reason we wanted to be like him. Now he _____ a good job in a good company, and in a few years he is going to work for himself. He _____ a big truck, and he will use it to transport iron pipes around Mexico. He got married one-and-a-half years ago, and now he _____ a good wife and a baby. They live in a good neighborhood with most of their friends close to their house. I _____ a special feeling for my brother because he _____ always taken care of me.

Marcelo Mendez
Mexico

II

My Father

My father is a very respectable man, but he has had a tough life. He has been overweight, and he _____ smoked three packs of cigarettes a day. So when he was 32 years old, he _____ a heart attack. After that, he worked very hard to quit smoking, but after one year he gave in to his addiction. Last May, at the young age of 41, he _____ his second heart attack. This led to emergency surgery and a quadruple-bypass operation. Being the strong man he is, Dad came through the surgery well. However, October 1st of this year brought even more grief. He found out that he _____ sugar diabetes. I believe that since my father has overcome all his other adversities, he will face this challenge successfully.

Brent Putchett
United States

> Make new friends, but keep old friends.
> One is silver, the other is gold.
> All of them are just like jewels.
> Age will mellow and refine them.
>
> translated by
> *Saud Degel*
> Saudi Arabia

POSSESSIVE ADJECTIVES

My mother	*His* father's name
Her sister's children	*Our* brother
Your cousin	*Their* parents

My Mother

MY mother's name is Maria de los Angeles Ramirez Enriquez. She is 52 years old, and she has black hair and brown eyes, the same as mine. HER first name, Maria, has a Catholic meaning. In Mexico it is a very common custom to use the names Maria and Guadalupe for women. MY mother's birthplace was Veracruz, a tropical state in Mexico that is close to the Gulf of Mexico. Now MY mother's home is in Mexico City, and she is a teacher in a primary school.

Raymundo Iturbe
Mexico

Exercise 1C

Read the paragraphs that follow. Write the TO BE verbs in the blanks. <u>Underline</u> the possessive adjectives. The first possessive adjective is <u>underlined</u> for you.

I

My Cousins

<u>**My**</u> three cousins and their families live in the U.S. Leonor, my oldest cousin, _____ 30 years old. She lives with her mother (my aunt) in a beautiful home in Washington, D.C. Leonor's brother _____ named German. He _____ a Catholic priest, and he made the celebration of my marriage. His church _____ in New York City. Oscar _____ my other cousin. He lives with his family in their large house in Houston, Texas. His daughter's name _____ Janet, and his son's name _____ Miguel.

Misela Marquez
Venezuela

II

My Father

My father _____ important in my life. All these years he has been my friend. When I _____ a small boy, he took me to my school. I _____ not afraid, and I learned as much as I could. All these years, his love for me has helped me in difficult moments. He has been beside me, telling me what to do. This year, I _____ going to study administration because my father wants me to study it. In the future, I will return to my home, and I will work there with my father.

Santiago Mendez
Venezuela

The duck's son is a swimmer.

translated by
Youssef El-Tayash
Libya

QUESTIONS

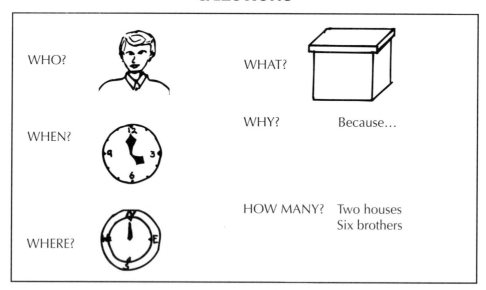

WHO?

WHEN?

WHERE?

WHAT?

WHY?   Because...

HOW MANY?   Two houses
            Six brothers

Writing Assignment

Look at the photograph on page 7. Read the information about the family. Then complete the paragraph that follows. Write the correct form of the verbs TO BE and TO HAVE in the blanks.

Moussa's Family

This _____ a picture of Moussa's family. Moussa _____ the
     be   **be**
father. He _____ not in the photo. Moussa's wife's name _____ Fati
     be   **be**
Mouss. She _____ 24 years old. Moussa _____ three children. Her
     be   **have**
older son _____ 5 years old. Yacoubor _____ his name. Moussa's
     be   **be**
younger son _____ 2 years old. His name _____ Issaka. Moussa's
     be   **be**
daughter _____ 3 years old. Her name _____ Kadi. Moussa and his
     be   **be**
family _____ from Niger.
     be

Moussa Hossane's Family from Niger
Older son: Yacoubor Hossane (5 years old)
Younger son: Issaka Hossane (2 years old)
Daughter: Kadi Hossane (3 years old)
Wife: Fati Mouss (24 years old)

SUBJECT AND OBJECT PRONOUNS

Subject	Object
I	me
you	you
he, she, it	him, her, it
we	us
you	you
they	them
this	this

My Mother
(His)

My mother is someone inside me. I can never forget her. She died, but she
(His)   **(him)(He)**

is both a sadness and an unforgettable smile in my life. She is a sadness because I
(his)   **(he)**

lost her, and she is a smile because she taught me so many things about life and
(him)

people. I can never forget her because she taught me the meaning of strength and
(He)   **(him)**

mercy. She was very strong with me whenever I did something wrong. But she was
(him)   **(he)**

very merciful when she saw me in a bad mood or when I was sick. I could always
(him)   **(he)**   **(He)**

see love in her eyes.

Abdullah Amirah
Saudi Arabia

NOTE: If Abdullah wrote the paragraph, he would use "I," "my," and "me." If his friend Ali writes the paragraph about Abdullah, Ali will use "he," "his," and "him."

Exercise 1D

With a partner, read the following paragraphs. Then do the exercises that follow each paragraph.

I

My Mother

I will tell you something about my mother. My mother's name is Lourdes Moncada. She is from Spain, but she has lived in Nicaragua, her husband's country, for 23 years. She is a tender woman. For example, when my sister and I are sleeping, she comes into our room, no matter what the hour, and she kisses us. She does the same thing every night. My mother helps people wherever they need her. One day, a poor boy came to our home with a big wound on his arm, and my mother cured him. However, when she gets angry, she really does. Last year my brother broke a living room lamp, and she made him buy a new one with his own money. Right now she is living in a small town with my father and her children.

Maria Lourdes Moncada
Nicaragua

1. <u>Underline</u> the subject pronouns in the paragraph (the first one, "I," is <u>underlined</u> for you).
2. Circle the possessive adjectives in the paragraph (the first one is circled for you).
3. Where was Maria's mother born?
4. How many times does Maria use the word "mother" in this paragraph?

II

My Mother's Feet

My mother, even though she is a normal mother, has something different from other mothers: her feet. Do not think that my mother is a monster. No! The difference is that my mother's feet are generally bigger than other mothers' feet, at least in my country. For example, when my mother goes to a shoe store in Colombia, she cannot find her size, which is usually bigger than the biggest shoe in the store. So, sometimes my mother's feet are a problem, not only for her, but also for me. The other day I had to buy a pair of "nice" shoes here in the United States to send to her. The problem was whether the shoes I chose were "nice" or not. They seemed nice to me, but I do not know if she really liked them. Usually my mother has to wait for nearly a month for her new shoes from the United States or from the factory. I tell my mother that she has "American feet."

Jorge Ramirez
Colombia

1. Underline 5 subject pronouns in paragraph II. The first one, "she," is underlined for you.
2. Circle 5 possessive adjectives in the paragraph.
3. What ONE idea is this paragraph about?
4. Write this paragraph about Jorge's mother again. Use "he," "his," and "him" instead of "I," "my," and "me."

Writing Assignment

Write the answers to the following questions about your family.

- What is your father's name?
- How old is your father?
- What is your father's job?
- What is your mother's name?
- What is your mother's job?
- Where do your parents live?
- How many sisters do you have?
- What are their names?
- How old are they?
- How many brothers do you have?
- What are their names?
- How old are they?

Next, exchange your answers with a partner. Write new answers to the questions. Use "his" and "him" instead of "my" and "mine." Then share your answers with your partner.

The Rose (a children's poem)

From the sky a rose fell down.
My grandmother picked it up.
She wore it on her head,
And how nice it was to look at.

translated by
John Shyh-Yuan Wang
China (P.R.C.)

CAPITAL LETTERS

Capitalize:

- the first letter of each sentence

- the first letter of the names of people, cities, countries

- the first letter of each word in a title

- The pronoun "I"

My Grandfather

My grandfather is the head of my family. His name is Tarik, the same as mine, and he is the oldest man in my family. He is smart, strong, and wise. He was a member of the Iraqi revolution against the English enemies during the First World War. He has lived a simple life with no cars, electricity, or television. When he was a young man, he traveled by horse, by camel, and by small boat. He needed strong nerves. Now he stays at our home, and he advises us.

Tarik Swadi Abdulsada
Iraq

Exercise 1E

Capitalize the appropriate words in the following paragraph. In the paragraph, 17 letters need to be capitalized.

my grandmother

my grandmother is different from me. she is short and fat and very white, but i am tall and thin and darker. she is beautiful, but i am not. her name is mahvash. she has a small view of the world because she is not well educated. for example, she does not know that other parts of the world have different types of lives and different religions. she never tries to learn new things. she is satisfied with her life in iran.

pavuin safari
iran

SUBJECT—VERB—COMPLEMENT

Subject	Verb	Complement
My mother	is	a traditional Chinese woman.
She	is	honest, hard-working, and patient.
She	has	black hair and brown eyes.
My father	needs	her every day.
Mother	encourages	her children to be courageous.
She	lives	in Taiwan with her family.
My mother	is	my teacher and my friend.

Julie Li-Chu Chung
Taiwan (R.O.C.)

Exercise 1F

*Make three columns on a piece of paper. Write **Subject, Verb**, and **Complement** at the top of the columns. Then write as many sentences as you can about your family in just three minutes. Share your sentences with a partner by reading your sentences aloud. Then listen to your partner's sentences. Finally, write one sentence about your partner's family that you remember.*

> A good neighbor is better than a brother who is far away.
>
> translated by
> *Kyu-Yong Lee*
> Korea

Exercise 1G

Read the following paragraphs. Circle the subject Ⓢ in each <u>underlined</u> sentence. Put a box around the verb Ⓥ in each sentence. Then do the exercises that follow each paragraph.

I

My Father

(My) father ⬚is⬚ the strongest person in our family, but he also has kindness and wisdom. <u>He was born at the beginning of the century.</u> <u>He grew up in a very hard environment.</u> As I grew up, I knew my father as a very loving and generous man. He taught us to be very polite. He encouraged our good behavior and good feelings toward each other. He believed that every one of his sons should be a man in his appearance and his behavior.

Ahmed Ghamdy
Saudi Arabia

1. ⃝Circle the possessive adjectives in the paragraph. The first possessive adjective, "My," has been circled for you.

2. What is this paragraph about?

3. Is there one main idea in the paragraph?

4. When was Ahmed's father born?

II

My Father

<u>The most important person in [my] life is my father</u>. (He) has been the example for me to develop my social and professional life. In my social life, he showed me how to be with people and what behavior I need to have in different situations. For example, I talk or behave differently with a director of a company than with a worker. My father could not study in school, but he has a lot of experience. <u>He is a good worker with high responsibilities in his work</u>. He also taught me that the most important responsibilities are to my work and my family.

<u>My father was a very good baseball player when he was young</u>. He likes all sports, and he taught me to play sports with a clear mind. <u>My father is an average person</u>. <u>However, he has been the biggest person for me</u>.

Juan Manuel Ortiz Mata
Mexico

1. Circle the subject (S) and put a box around the verb [V] in the <u>underlined</u> sentences.

2. Put brackets [ ] around 5 possessive adjectives. The first one is completed for you.

3. Put parentheses ( ) around 5 subject pronouns. The first one is completed for you.

4. What has Juan learned from his father?

III

Thrifty Mother

My mother is very thrifty, and that _____ very important for our family happiness. If my mother wants to buy something, usually she checks the prices from several places before she decides where she wants to shop. Sometimes the difference of the price _____ not too much, but she likes to spend her time bargaining. <u>By doing that, my mother saves some of her daily expenses</u>. On special occasions, like birthdays, my mother can make a special party without asking for additional money from my father. When my father _____ not at home, my mother can solve unexpected problems by using her savings from daily expenses. <u>For example, sometimes our family needs extra money to go to the doctor or to buy medicine</u>. My mother's thrifty ways _____ helpful for all of my family.

Juliardi Kahar
Indonesia

1. Write the correct verb TO BE in the blanks.

2. Circle the subject (S) and put a box around the verb [V] in the <u>underlined</u> sentences.

3. Can you guess the meaning of "thrifty" from the underlined sentences in the paragraph?

4. Why is Juliardi's mother "special"?

Writing Assignment

List details about <u>one</u> quality of <u>one</u> of your parents. For example, is your mother thrifty? an excellent cook? a good teacher? Is your father generous? intelligent? a good teacher? Then give an example for each quality. Use the chart below to plan your paragraph.

PARAGRAPH PLANNING

My mother (father) is	**For example,**
_____	_____
_____	_____
_____	_____
_____	_____

Next, write a paragraph about one of your parents. Share that paragraph with your partner. As you read your partner's paragraph, <u>underline</u> the most interesting example. Then tell your partner why you liked that example.

THE PARAGRAPH

Title

(indent)
⟶   A paragraph is a group of sentences about ONE MAIN IDEA. Usually the title and the first sentence of the paragraph tell the main idea of the paragraph. The first sentence of the paragraph is indented. Each sentence in the paragraph begins with a capital letter. All the sentences in the paragraph have a subject and a verb. Each sentence ends with a period (.).

Writing Assignment

Look at the photograph of a family. With a partner, write a paragraph about the photo. Answer some of the following questions:

- Who is this family?

- Where is the family from?

- How many people are in the family?

- How many daughters?

- How many children are in the family?

- How many sons?

- How old are the people in the family?

- What are the names of the people in the family?

The Family of Ryu Ki Hee from Korea
Father: Ryu Ki Hee (32 years old)
Mother: Park Jung Sook (31 years old)
Older son: Ryu Dae Kue (7 years old)
Younger son: Ryu Shin Kue (6 years old)

Exercise 1H

Read the following paragraphs. Then do the exercises that follow each paragraph.

I

My Cousin

My best friend is named Federico, and he is also my cousin. Federico and I are the same age, but he is taller than I am. He has dark, curly hair and blue eyes. We studied together in elementary school, in high school, and at the same university. We spent much time together, talking about problems in our lives. We never had a fight. We always tried to help each other. In high school, we enjoyed playing a sport called *toros coleados* which is practiced with horses and bulls. <u>Federico is also a good guitar player</u>. Now, when I hear someone playing a guitar, I think of my good friend.

Mario Martinez
Venezuela

1. (Circle) the subject (S) in the <u>underlined</u> sentences.
2. Put a box around the verb [V] in the <u>underlined</u> sentences.
3. What is the main idea in this paragraph?
4. Why does Mario think about Federico when he hears guitar music?

II

My Mother's Cooking

When I lived at home, I loved the delicious food my mother fixed. She is interested in fixing a traditional food called upside-downs. The food contains meat and rice and potatoes. It _____ a good smell and taste, and I could smell it from a long distance. I could pick the dish my mother fixed from many other dishes because she _____ special experience. In addition, she always makes noises when she prepares the food, like the noise of the spoons and dishes. When I heard that noise, I became impatient and hungry. As long as I was at home, I never missed my mother's food. But now I miss it every day. I will always remember my mother's food as long as I live.

Basem Masaedeh
Saudi Arabia

1. What is the main idea of this paragraph?
2. Draw the arrow (——→) to show the indentation of the first sentence of the paragraph.
3. Write the correct verb TO HAVE in the blanks.
4. (Circle) the period at the end of each sentence.

Writing Assignment

Write a paragraph about ONE special person in your family (your mother? your cousin? your brother? your grandfather?). First, answer the questions below. Next, complete the planning chart below. Then write the paragraph.

- Who is the person?

- What does he or she look like?

- How old is he or she?

- Why are you writing about this person?

- What makes this person "special"?

- Has the person influenced you?

- In what ways?

- Use the chart below to help plan your paragraph.

PLANNING CHART

Adjectives	How do you know?
warm, loving	She smiles a lot.
understanding	He listens to my problems.
helpful	She tries to help her friends.
generous	_____
_____	_____
_____	_____
_____	_____
_____	_____

Next, share your paragraph with a partner. Read your partner's paragraph. Tell your partner what was most interesting about her/his parent.

If there is a well in a dry field,
we will take a bath.
If God spares our lives,
we will meet again.

translated by
Hadi Pasaribu
Indonesia

MY FAMILY

Exercise 1I

Read the following paragraphs. Then do the exercises that follow each paragraph.

I

_____

my first name, sakda, was the name of a man who was well known by people in my country, thailand. in 1939 he was the only soldier who escaped from the battle with the communists in the jungle. my first name means "a man who has power and strength." so my first name is a special name in thai. my last name, wattanasupt, was given by the seventh king of thailand. in my country, most of my friends call me "aye" because thai people don't like to say long names. also, short nicknames like aye show the close relationship between my friends and me.

sakda wattanasupt
thailand

1. Capitalize the appropriate words in the paragraph. 18 words need to be capitalized.

2. Write a title for this paragraph. Be sure to capitalize the first letter of each word in your title.

3. Circle 5 TO BE verbs in this paragraph. The first TO BE is completed for you.

4. Why is the writer called "Aye"?

II

Some Things About My Name

The Venezuelan people have a custom that every child be called by four names: two first names and two last names. My last names are from my mother's side and my father's side of the family. Therefore, my complete name is Hilda Zulema Gonzalez Cruz. My first name, Hilda, is the same as my mother's first name. My father wanted to give me my mother's name because I am the first and only daughter after four sons. My second name, Zulema, has a curious history. When my mother was pregnant, she listened to a famous novel on the radio, called Prince Tamacun. In this novel there were two princesses: Arelis and Zulema. My parents asked my older brother what name he preferred, Arelis or Zulema. He chose Zulema. It is a name from Arabia. Gonzalez, my third name, is very common in my country. It is from my father. Finally, my last name, Cruz, is from the Canary Islands. This name was given to my mother's family by my great-great-grandfather.

Zulema Gonzalez
Venezuela

1. (Circle) the subject (S) and put a box around the verb [V] in the underlined sentences.

2. Put parentheses ( ) around 8 possessive adjectives.

3. How many times does Zulema use the word "name(s)" in the paragraph? Why do you think she used that word so many times?

4. Change the pronouns "I" and "my" to "she" and "her" in this paragraph.

Interview

Ask your partner some of the questions below. Write the answers to the questions. Use the correct subject pronouns. Then introduce your classmate to the other people in your class.

- What is your name?

- What country are you from?

- How old are you?

- Are you married?

- Do you have children?

- Do you live alone?

- What is your major?

- How long have you been in the U.S.?

Do not ignore small things because they have their uses. For example, a sword is useless when a needle is needed.

translated by
Dattatray Vaidankar
India

Exercise 1J

With a partner, read the following paragraphs. Then do the exercises that follow each paragraph.

I

My Name

My name is Hu Cheng-Hwa. Hu is not my first name. It is my family name. The family name is first in the traditional Chinese style. In the U.S., many people are not able to pronounce my family name correctly. In Chinese, "Hu" is quite different from "Who," but the sounds in English are not different. Most people in Taiwan call me "Lau-Hu." *Lau* means "old." However, in Chinese, the meaning is not "old" when someone calls his friend "Lau." It is just for friendship. Cheng-Hwa is my given name. *Cheng* means "real," "true." *Hwa* means Chinese. So my name means "really Chinese." Of course, I am not able to write my name in the Chinese style in the U.S. Therefore, my name here is Cheng-Hwa Hu.

Cheng-Hwa Hu
Taiwan (R.O.C.)

1. What is the main idea of this paragraph?
2. Circle the subject Ⓢ and put a box around the verb ⃞V⃞ in the underlined sentences.
3. Put brackets [ ] around 5 possessive adjectives.
4. Why can't people in the U.S. pronounce Hu's name?

II

My Name

My first name is a Spanish one: Fernando. In my country, it is traditional to choose the child's first name (or names) from among his ancestors' first names. It is also good to include the name of a saint to protect the child. A lucky child can have three or four names. I was not lucky. My brothers and cousins had used all the ancestors' names, so I did not have a saint to protect me. My mother chose Fernando because this was the name of Spanish kings. She believed that her family had very pure Spanish blood. My last name is Arango, and it is the last name of all my ancestors from my father's line. This name originated in a Spanish province called Aragon. Perhaps one foolish ancestor changed the spelling, and instead of Aragon, he wrote Arango!

Fernando Arango
Colombia

1. What is the main idea of this paragraph?
2. Circle the subject Ⓢ and put a box around the verb ⃞V⃞ in the underlined sentences.
3. Why was Fernando not "lucky"?
4. How many times does the writer use the word "name(s)"? Why?

Writing Assignment

Answer the questions below. Next, write a paragraph about your name. Remember to indent. Make your paragraph interesting for your partner. Then exchange paragraphs with your partner. As you read your partner's paragraph, underline the most interesting sentence in the paragraph. Then tell your partner why you found that sentence interesting.

- What is your complete name?
- What does each of your names mean?
- Why did your parents give you your name(s)?
- What is special about your name?
- Is there anything amusing about your name?

> If you work harder and harder, you'll get results.
>
> translated by
> *Mohamud Fahie*
> Somalia

Exercise 1K

With your partner, read the following paragraphs. Then do the exercises that follow each paragraph.

I

My Name

My name is Jun Wang, Eric. Jun is my first name. Wang is my second name. Usually, a Chinese name includes three parts: first, second, and last. However, I do not have a second name. In Chinese, *Jun*, my first name, means "a great strong white horse who can run rapidly, 10,000 miles a day." Chinese people always use the word "*Jun*" to encourage someone to reach a goal. My last name, *Wang*, means "king" in Chinese. According to Chinese tradition, the hope of my future is explained by my name. Unfortunately, I found a problem when I came to the U.S. My first name was not clear to people because it is similar to June, which is a girl's name and the name of a summer month. For this reason, I have been given an American name, Eric, that also means "king."

Jun Wang
China (P.R.C.)

1. Circle the subject (S) and put a box around the verb [V] in the underlined sentences.
2. Put parentheses ( ) around the TO BE and TO HAVE verbs.

3. Why does Jun have a North American name?
4. Why was he named Eric?

II

Marysol Coromoto Rangel Martinez de Berti

Marysol, my first name, is derived from the Spanish name, Maria. This is for the Virgin Mary. In Spanish, soledad means "lonely." But my wonderful parents did not like that meaning. Therefore, they named me Marysol. *Mar* means "sea," and *sol* means "sun." A problem came when I was baptized because Marysol was not a religious name. So my parents also gave me the name Coromoto, after a saint who lived in the nineteenth century in Venezuela. I have three last names. The first, Rangel, is my father's. It originated in Spain, and then it became an Indian name in the Andes, the region where my father was born. My second name, Martinez, is my mother's maiden name. It also came from Spain, and afterwards from the region in Venezuela called Aragua. Finally, I have a married name. In my country, when a woman marries, she adds the term *de* and her husband's name. The *de* means she is *de*pendent on her husband. My husband's name, Berti, is from Italy, from the island of Elba. It is a name of noble origin.

Marysol Rangel de Berti
Venezuela

1. Circle the subject (S) and put a box around the verb [V] in the underlined sentences.

2. Put parentheses ( ) around the TO BE and TO HAVE verbs.

3. Put brackets [ ] around 6 subject pronouns.

4. What does the name Marysol mean in English?

To those who stand under a good tree,
a good shadow nurtures them.

translated by
Olga Handal
Honduras

Writing Assignment

With a partner, look at the photographs on pages 24 and 25. Choose one photograph. Next, with your partner, write one paragraph about the family in that photograph. Answer some of the questions that are listed. Then make up some details to make the paragraph more interesting.

- Why did you choose this photograph?
- How many people are in the family?
- How many children are in the family?
- How old is each person in the family?
- How many sons are in the family? How many daughters?
- What does the father look like?
- What does the mother look like?
- What does each child look like?
- Where is the family from?
- What are the names of the people in the family?

Then, share your paragraph with another pair of partners. Discuss the details that make the other paragraph interesting.

The Family of Bonar Siregar from Indonesia
Father: Bonar Siregar (45 years old)
Mother: N. Sitorus (42 years old)
Older son: Ivan (14 years old)
Older daughter: Imelda (13 years old)
Younger daughter: Indra (12 years old)
Younger son: Ivo (8 years old)

The Family of Hiroyuki Nakama from Japan
Father: Hiroyuki Nakama (38 years old)
Mother: Noriko Nakama (37 years old)
Older daughter: Ayano Nakama (14 years old)
Younger daughter: Hiroko Nakama (6 years old)

Other Writing Topics

My Friend

My Teacher

My Sister's (Brother's) Name

My Neighbor

My Sister's (Brother's) Friend

Writing Projects

Individual Writing Project: Write several paragraphs about the people in your family. The titles of your paragraphs might be:

My Mother

My Father

My Grandmother

My Grandfather

My Oldest Sister (Brother)

My Youngest Brother (Sister)

My Brothers (Sisters)

My Cousin(s)

In each paragraph, answer some of these questions:

• What is her or his name?

• Where does she or he live?

- What is her or his job?

- What does she or he look like?

- Why is she or he special?

- Is she or he married?

- Is she or he studying?

- What do you remember about her or him?

- How has she or he influenced you?

- Do you remember an interesting story about her or him?

- Do you remember an amusing story about her or him?

When you have finished the paragraphs, make a booklet. Use photographs of your family to make the booklet more interesting. Use construction paper and staples or brads to fasten the booklet together. Decorate the front of the booklet with the title and other art work. Display the booklets in your classroom, and invite another class to come to your class and read the booklets.

Group Writing Project: <u>Ask</u> friends who are NOT in your class to write paragraphs about their names. Or, <u>interview</u> several friends about their names, and write paragraphs about those names.

Gather all the paragraphs together. Exchange your paragraphs with a partner. Correct any errors you find (ask your teacher for advice). Then tell your partner which paragraph(s) you found most interesting. Put the paragraphs into a booklet. Make copies of the booklet for all the students who contributed paragraphs.

2

Home

My Hometown

Alexandria is the second biggest city in my country, Egypt, and I live in this city. It is a beautiful city, and people there are very kind and polite. Tourists like to visit my city because it is on the sea. When I walk down the Kornash, the largest street, I see the beautiful blue sea and sky, and the beautiful green grass and trees. In the spring, the flowers grow in many colors: yellow, red, and blue. The most beautiful scene is the white birds. In the winter, a very big flock of birds migrates to this place. I watch them while they skillfully fish from the sea. The birds watch the fish, and they wait patiently for a long time. When the fish come to the surface, they fly quickly and catch them. In the fall, the city looks like a very old man because the leaves of the trees fall from the trees. That is my city, and I think it is the most beautiful city in the world.

Abdelmegig Fahmy
Egypt

PRESENT TENSE VERBS (every day, a habit)

Subject		Verb	Complement
I		talk	to my mother.
He	Ali *OR* Abdul	live**s**	in Egypt.
She	Marta *OR* Hussa	write**s**	letters to her friends
It	The river *OR* The stream	flow**s**	through the village.
You	Mahmoud and Sylvia	help	the new students.
We	Tarig, Mariana, and Kumi	come	to class every day.
They	Lucas and Parvin	drink	tea at breakfast.

EXAMPLES OF PRESENT TENSE VERBS

come(s)	help(s)	rise(s)	stand(s)
drink(s)	is (are)	run(s)	start(s)
feel(s)	like(s)	speak(s)	think(s)
find(s)	live(s)	spend(s)	walk(s)
give(s)	put(s)	spread(s)	write(s)

My Hometown

The city I LIVE in is called Haifa. Haifa is a beautiful city with a magnificent panorama. It STARTS at the Mediterranean Sea, CONTINUES with a flat area that ENDS at the slopes of the Carmel Mountains. I LIVE about half way up the mountain, and I HAVE a beautiful view spreading below. The house I LIVE in is in an apartment building with a red roof. I LIVE on the upper floor.

Shoshana Zachs
Israel

Night falls, darkness spreads.
The wind, surging through the fields
Brings my thoughts home.

translated by
Sin S. Chiu
Hong Kong

Exercise 2A

Read the paragraphs that follow. Some present tense verbs are <u>underlined</u>. Circle *the subject for each <u>underlined</u> present tense verb. The first subject is circled for you.*

I

My City

My city, Huanzheu, <u>is</u> a famous beautiful city in China, and it <u>is</u> famous all over the world too. It <u>is</u> set between the river and West Lake. Several hills <u>spread</u> around West Lake, and some mountains <u>stand</u> by the river. These <u>give</u> the city many beautiful scenes, and so Huanzheu <u>is</u> famous for its beauty. It <u>is</u> beautiful in the spring when the trees bud green and the peach trees flower with their red blossoms. It <u>is</u> beautiful in the summer when the lilies <u>float</u> in the lake. It <u>is</u> beautiful in the fall when the leaves <u>turn</u> yellow and red. And it <u>is</u> beautiful in the winter when the snow gives white clothes to the mountains. So Huanzheu <u>is</u> beautiful all year. It <u>is</u> beautiful when the sunshine <u>is</u> bright because the hills <u>make</u> shadows in the lake. It <u>is</u> beautiful when the rain <u>falls</u> and makes the frogs rise from the lake. My city <u>is</u> always beautiful.

Dong Aichu
China (P.R.C.)

II

My Hometown

My hometown, Chia-Yi, <u>is</u> located in southwest Taiwan. It <u>is</u> mostly surrounded by plains that produce rice, but the region also <u>grows</u> fruit. Because it <u>is</u> in a subtropical zone, it <u>produces</u> fruit all year. Mango, pineapple, and papaya <u>are</u> my favorite fruits in the summertime, and I <u>enjoy</u> oranges, grapes, and bananas during our short "winter." We can always get fresh vegetables and fruit at very reasonable prices. Because they <u>are</u> so fresh, they <u>taste</u> delicious. Now that I <u>am</u> far away from Chia-Yi, I often <u>think</u> of a Chinese poem:

> After I <u>lift</u> up my head.
> to see the brilliant moon,
> I <u>lower</u> my head
> and think of my hometown.
>
> *Chia-Chu Dorland*
> Taiwan (R.O.C.)

Exercise 2B

With a partner, read the following paragraphs. In each blank (_____), write the correct present tense form of the verb.

I

My Small Town

Soba is a small town in my country, Sudan. It _____ 120 kilometers
be

from Khartoum, the capital of Sudan. The Nile River _____ through Soba.
flow

That _____ the town green and beautiful.   Most of the people in
make

Soba _____ as farmers or fishermen. The Nile is very important in their
work

lives. A small market in Soba _____ food to the people who cannot go to the
sell

market in the capital.   In Soba, a small hospital and a pharmacy _____
give

medicine to the people without money. About 50 percent of the people in Soba

_____ in the hospital. The youth club in Soba _____ the youth a place
work   **give**

to meet every night except Friday. Friday _____ a holy day in Soba, so the
be

people _____ to the mosque, and they _____ their prayers. The people
go   **say**

in Soba _____ their town. They _____ very happy because Soba is
love   **be**

crowded with beautiful things.

Shiek Idris Mahmoud Hassan
Sudan

II

My Hometown

Taipei, the city where I _____ , is the most beautiful city I have ever
live

seen. It is located among the mountains—Yun Ming San, Chi-Sing San, Wi-Ji San,

and Gun-In San—so the air around the city _____ very fresh. Many rivers
be

_____ through the city, so the scenery is beautiful. The buildings _____
flow   **be**

traditional Chinese style. I never _____ lonely because there are so many
feel

places to enjoy myself. About 70 theaters, 100 galleries, 10 museums, and 5

gymnasiums, _____ the people busy. I _____ Chinese food, so I
keep   **like**

_____ Taipei. There are about 3,000 Chinese restaurants there, and the food
love

they _____ is very delicious and fresh.
serve

Chi-Chang Wang
Taiwan (R.O.C.)

Writing Assignment

Write a paragraph about your hometown. Answer some of the following questions.

- What is the name of your hometown?
- Where is it?
- How large (or how small) is it?
- What does your hometown look like?
- What is the weather in your hometown?
- What makes your hometown beautiful?
- What makes your hometown special?

Next, share your paragraph with a partner. After you have read your partner's paragraph, ask your partner some questions about his or her hometown. Then, answer your partner's questions about your hometown.

Now, write your paragraph again. Include the new information your partner asked you about. Finally, share your new paragraph with your partner.

Song of Returning Home

So young was I when I left home.
So old am I when I come back.
My native accent doesn't change,
though my hair has turned white.
Children see me but don't know me.
Smiling, they ask where I come from.

translated by
Prayat Laopropassone
Thailand

PRESENT TENSE SPELLING (He, She, It + Present Tense)*

	Regular	Verbs that end in -sh, -ch, -ss, and -x	Verbs that end in vowel + y		Verbs that end in consonant + y	
	smile**s**	brush**es**	pay	pay**s**	study	stud**ies**
	walk**s**	wash**es**	buy	buy**s**	worry	worr**ies**
HE	close**s**	teach**es**	enjoy	enjoy**s**	carry	carr**ies**
SHE	speak**s**	watch**es**				
IT	say**s**	kiss**es**				
	look**s**	toss**es**				
	drive**s**	relax**es**				
	turn**s**					
	work**s**					
	look**s**					

*See Appendices C and D for spelling rules.

Exercise 2C

Read the following paragraphs. With a partner, choose the correct present tense verb from the list below each paragraph. Write the correct form of each present tense verb in the blank (_____). Use each verb on the list only once.

I

Jubeal

My country, Lebanon, is all beautiful, but one city _____ more beautiful than the others. Jubeal is the small city where I _____. On one side of the city, the golden sand of the beach beside the sea reflects the sunlight like a colored mirror. In the summer, people fill the beach. They _____ the sunlight, and they _____ in the sea. Away from the sea, the mountains _____ in the middle of the city. Their green trees and grasses _____ the people in Jubeal happy. From these mountains, rivers _____ into the city. The sounds of the rivers are like melodies in heaven. All these things make Jubeal a beautiful place.

VERBS: enjoy swim be make live rise flow

Mustapha Ghaddar
Lebanon

II

Wind Blowing Free

Thirty miles from the edge of the world, where the wind always _____ , there is a quiet little town called Ten Sleep, Wyoming. "Two blinks" means that if you blink more than twice while you are driving through, you will miss the town. The population of Ten Sleep is 370 when my friends and I are gone, and 378 when we return. Ten Sleep _____ a gas station, a store, a restaurant, and, of course, two bars. The town doesn't mean much to most people, but to me it is my home and my life. For example, it is always quiet and peaceful when I most need it, but if I am ready to have some fun, I can always find my friends in no time at all. Ten Sleep is a place where children grow up learning how to work hard and play even harder. Nobody locks their doors, and I can walk down the street at any time of day or night and feel completely safe. A typical summer day involves getting up at 7 A.M. to set irrigation lines on our ranch. Then my friends and I _____ on top of the hill and relax, enjoying the cool breeze and bright sunshine. We might decide to float in inner tubes on the creek that runs through town or to rope cows for fun. In Ten Sleep, everything _____ as simple and true as life should be. It is the place I love, and I _____ to return when I am finished with my university studies.

VERBS: have be plan blow meet

Robert Stine
United States

III

My Hometown

I _____ that one of the most beautiful cities in my country is Villavicencio. It _____ a typical Colombian country town. Near the town are many farms and cows, and often the farmers _____ parties like North American rodeos. People in the town _____ Villavicencio "the door of the jungle" because the jungle is very near the town. Many tourists _____ to Villavicencio because there are beautiful places to visit and many things to do. For example, the Andes Mountains _____ behind the city, and they are very beautiful. Many rivers _____ near the city. I _____ fishing to a different river almost every day. There are also many places for hunting in the jungle and in the mountains.

VERBS: be   have   think   flow   call   go   rise   come

Jorge Cano
Colombia

Each year for three hundred and sixty years
the cutting wind and biting frost contend.
How long can beauty flower fresh and fair?
In a single day wind can whirl it to its end.

translated by
Xirong Wei
China (P.R.C.)

Writing Assignment

Write a paragraph about another beautiful city in your country. Answer some of the questions that follow.

- What is the name of the city?
- Where is it located?
- How large (or small) is it?
- In what ways is it beautiful?
- Why do you like the city?
- When do you like to visit the city? Why?

THERE IS/THERE ARE

There is	+	SUBJECT	+	(COMPLEMENT)
There is		*a beautiful park*		*(in my hometown)*
There are	+	SUBJECT	+	(COMPLEMENT)
There are		*many parks*		*(in my hometown)*

My Home

My family's earthen home stands on the peak of a hill, giving a view of my home city. It is a seven-meter-square building with a straw roof. The four walls are painted a traditional gray. THERE IS a large yard for the family's leisure time. My father planted a grass lawn, and my mother grows flowers in the garden. The interior of my home has seven rooms. THERE ARE five bedrooms, a large combined dining and living room, and a bathroom.

Yenyou Bangole
Gabon

The horse, the night, and the desert know me,
the sword, the spear, the paper and pencil, too.

translated by
Sami Lazghah
Tunisia

Exercise 2D

With a partner, read the following paragraphs. Then do the exercises that follow.

I

My Home

My home is a small cement and brick house in Guayaquil, the biggest city in my country. It _____ located in a nice neighborhood, but there are some old houses around it. My house _____ three bedrooms, a kitchen, two bathrooms, a living room, a dining room, and a service room. There is enough room for my parents, my two brothers, my sisters, and a maid. Outside my house there is a beautiful garden with many flowers. There is also a garage for two cars. Now that I am studying in the United States and my sister _____ married, my house will seem a little bigger than it really is.

Gustavo Garcia
Ecuador

1. Write the correct TO BE and TO HAVE verbs in the blanks.

2. Underline THERE IS and THERE ARE in the paragraph. Circle the subject for each THERE IS/THERE ARE.

3. Why does Gustavo's house seem larger now? Have you had a similar experience?

4. What do you remember about Gustavo's house?

II

My Home

In Saudi Arabia, we _____ some restrictions about the sexes. Men and women _____ separate living areas. Therefore, we _____ two living rooms, two dining rooms, and several visitors' rooms. Of course, we also _____ separate bathrooms, bedrooms, and kitchens. My house _____ two entrances as well, one for men and the other for women. I live in a very big villa. It is brown and beige. The villa _____ six bedrooms, five bathrooms, two kitchens, two living rooms, one drawing room, and one garage.

Adel Salamah
Saudi Arabia

1. Write the correct form of the TO HAVE verbs in each blank.

2. Circle the subject in each sentence.

3. Why does Adel's house have two kitchens and two entrances?

4. Rewrite this paragraph. Use "he," "they," and "his" instead of "I," "we," and "my." Remember to change the verb to agree with its new subject:

I live ⟶ he lives

III

_____

Since Hong Kong is well known for its population density, skyscrapers instead of houses and flats are the most common buildings that can be found. The building I live in _____ ten floors, and my apartment _____ on the ninth floor. Two elevators take people up and down, and each floor _____ eight apartments. The rooms inside, though small in size, _____ comfortable and well furnished. There is a sitting room where our family enjoys life. We _____ a television set, a radio, and a tape recorder. After dinner, when everyone has finished his own work, we gather in the sitting room and listen to records or watch television. Since we are no longer children, we do not quarrel with each other, especially when our parents _____ present!

Alice Lo
Hong Kong

1. Write the correct form of the TO BE and TO HAVE verbs in each blank.

2. Underline THERE IS. Circle the subject for THERE IS.

3. Write a title for this paragraph.

4. What makes Alice's home different from the other students' homes described in paragraphs I and II?

The Rice Fields

The rice fields are carved in the mountain slope,
fenced in by a row of hills as far as the eye can see.
The new rice is all dressed in green.
The young maiden in her little hut is weaving
while watching over the rice fields.
Once in a while I hear her chant
a song straight from her heart.

translated by
Irawati Gregory
Indonesia

Writing Assignment

Write a paragraph about your house. Use some of these questions to plan your paragraph.

• What does your house look like from the outside?

• What does the yard around your house look like?

- What does your house look like inside?
- What things make your house special?
- What is your favorite room in your house? Why?

Next, share your paragraph with a partner. After you have read your partner's paragraph, ask your partner some questions about his or her house. Then, answer your partner's questions about your home.

Now, write your paragraph again. Include the new information your partner asked you about. Finally, share your new paragraph with your partner.

> Although I have to say goodbye,
> I want you to remember me forever, forever.
> Instead of wishing you happiness,
> I'm giving a forget-me-not to you.
>
> > translated by
> > *Yoko Fukuda*
> > Japan

ADVERBS OF FREQUENCY*

100% ◄────────		50% ───────		──────► 0%	
always	usually	often	sometimes	rarely	never

Examples of Adverbs of Frequency

SUBJECT	+	TO BE	+	frequency adverb	+	COMPLEMENT
I		am		**always**		homesick

OR

SUBJECT	+	frequency adverb	+	TO HAVE	+	COMPLEMENT
Libya		**usually**		has		hot weather

OR

SUBJECT	+ frequency adverb	+	OTHER VERBS	+	COMPLEMENT
She	**often**		misses		her brother

*NOTE: Placement of adverbs of frequency changes in some sentences.

What I Miss About My Country

I came to the U.S. only three weeks ago. However, I miss my family very much because I lived with them for twenty years, and I saw them every day. But now I NEVER see them. I also miss Libyan food. I USUALLY cannot find food from my country in the U.S., and I especially miss Libyan coffee. I miss looking at the beach, and I miss the beautiful weather. U.S. weather is different from weather in my country. In Libya the weather is always sunny in the summer, and in the winter it is USUALLY not cold. I miss my friends because I SOMETIMES studied with them. We OFTEN took trips together, and they OFTEN visited me. I miss my university too. I miss the library and my teachers. I hope to like the U.S. after I live here a long time.

Mnani-Ely Taiem
Libya

Exercise 2E

With a small group of classmates (three to five) in a circle, take turns saying sentences with adverbs of frequency. Speak quickly, and make up sentences about any topic. Everyone should have at least five turns.

Loneliness

Crow weeps to the dark.
Tide billows in the north wind.
How lonesome the world.

John Shyh-Yuan Wang
China (P.R.C.)

Exercise 2F

Individually, or with a partner, read the following paragraphs. Then do the exercises that follow each paragraph.

I

Sadness

I miss many things about my country such as my family, the food, and my friends. Living in the U.S. is difficult because I never have anybody to share my thoughts and experiences. In Venezuela, I used to be with my family every day. Now I am never with them, and it is very hard for me. For example, I often have problems with U.S. food because I am not accustomed to eating hamburgers. I never ate hamburgers before I came to the U.S.A. However, I cannot find typical

Venezuelan food in the supermarkets, so I sometimes eat hamburgers. My mother often sends me food from home such as coffee and *arepas.* One more thing I miss about my country is the language. I never hear Spanish. I do not have any friends here because I do not speak English. Therefore, I am always sad now because I miss my country so much.

Evelyn Rios
Venezuela

1. <u>Underline</u> 8 adverbs of frequency in the paragraph.

2. Circle the verb that comes before or after the adverbs of frequency.

3. Why is Evelyn sad? Have you had a similar experience?

4. Why does Evelyn's mother send her Venezuelan food?

II

—————————————

When my husband decided to come to the U.S., I was very happy because I thought the life in this country might be wonderful. I never studied English before I arrived, and this was my first and biggest difficulty. After a short time, when I realized I was not able to learn quickly, I told my husband, "I want to go back to Italy." Later, I decided to stay with my husband, but I am often sad and homesick. I miss my house, my friends, my relatives, and particularly my nephew. His name is Marco, and he is four years old. When my husband first went to the U.S.A., and I remained in Italy, Marco was angry with him. Marco told me, "Aunt Ginetta, you must look for another husband. I will be your husband!" I don't have any children, and I love Marco like a son. When I write a letter to my family, I always put, "Dear Marco, wait for me. I'm going to return to you soon. I send you my kisses."

Ginetta Longato
Italy

1. Put parentheses ( ) around 3 adverbs of frequency in the paragraph.

2. Circle the verb that comes before or after each adverb of frequency.

3. Write a title for this paragraph.

4. Whom does Ginetta particularly miss?

III

Why I Miss My Family

My country is one of the smaller countries in Europe, and it _____
be
really quiet. I rarely _____ my country because I _____ the U.S.A., but
miss **like**
I sometimes _____ about Swiss cheese, Swiss chocolate, and Swiss fondue! I
think
miss my family above all. My mother _____ really nice, and I don't say that
be
just because she's my mum. She's more than a mother for me. She's my best friend.

Before I left Switzerland, she told me, "Don't worry about me, and be happy." I also

miss my uncle. He _____ like a brother to me, and I can always laugh with
be
him. My grandmother _____ as sweet as her cakes. I love her cakes, and I
be
_____ her, too. She always _____ about other people and never about
love **think**
herself. I miss her. Finally, I miss my cat Zorro. Do you think it's crazy to miss a

cat? Perhaps. But I can't change my mind. I miss Zorro. My family isn't a special

family, but it's my own family, and I miss everyone!

Annick Burkhalter
Switzerland

1. Write the correct present tense form of the verbs in the blanks.
2. (Circle) the subject for each of the verbs in the blanks.
3. Underline 5 frequency adverbs.
4. What is amusing about this paragraph?

IV

East or West, Home Is Best

I miss my country so much. Every day I think about the sea and the sun. In

my country, I always _____ to the sea to play and relax. I _____ the
go **spend**
whole summer in the sun. But in the United States, there is no beach, and I never

have time to relax. I also miss my home and my family. I _____ the evenings
miss
we spent together, miss watching TV and drinking tea. I miss these things because

here I do not have a close friend, and I do not have a family. Here we _____
have
dinner at five o'clock. In Libya, we usually have dinner at one o'clock, so the family

_____ tea at five o'clock. Everything _____ different here, even the
have **be**
time of dinner. Finally, I miss my university so much, and I miss my friends there.

Every Friday, my friends and I always had a small party. I miss that party a lot. I

miss everything about my country.

Nurelhuda Ali Bassuine
Libya

1. Write the correct present tense form of the verbs in the blanks.
2. Underline 4 adverbs of frequency. Circle the verbs that come before *or* after the frequency adverbs.
3. Put a box around THERE IS . Put brackets [ ] around the subject of THERE IS.
4. What advice would you give to Nurelhuda to help her be happier?

Migratory Bird

Bird, are you leaving?
Fly me to your home with you
on your feathered back.

translated by
T. Kim
Korea

Interview

Ask a classmate the following questions. Write the answers to the questions. Use adverbs of frequency in your sentences.

- What do you always miss about your hometown?

- What do you usually miss about your hometown?

- What do you often miss about your hometown?

- What do you sometimes miss about your hometown?

- What do you rarely miss about your hometown?

- What do you never miss about your hometown?

- What do you have to do every day? (Always)

- What do you usually have to do?

- What do you often have to do?

- What do you sometimes have to do?

- What do you rarely have to do?

- What do you never have to do?

Now, rewrite the answers to your questions. Change the *he/she, his/hers,* and *him/her* to *I, me,* and *my*. Be sure that the verbs you use agree with the subjects.

> Why can't I wave it away?
> Why can't I erase it?
> I miss my hometown, and
> I feel sad to recall the people there
> A thousand million miles away,
> When will we be able to get together?
>
> translated by
> *Chia-Chon Pin*
> Taiwan (R.O.C.)

Writing Assignment

Write a paragraph about one person (or one place, or one thing) in your country that you miss. Answer some of the questions in the following chart.

What I Miss About My Country

What or Who?	Why?
_____	because _____ .
	because _____ .
	because _____ .

1. Make a list of ideas for your paragraph.

2. Begin to write your paragraph. Try to use interesting details.

3. Exchange paragraphs with a partner.

4. After you read your partner's paragraph, ask your partner two to four questions about the ideas in the paragraph that will help your partner make his or her paragraph more interesting.

5. Now, rewrite your paragraph. Include the new information that your partner asked about.

6. In a small group of classmates, read several paragraphs. Discuss with your group which paragraph you thought was most interesting.

Come from far away, stay with me.
You're my glorious sun.
You must stay, don't ask me why.
Stay and destroy all the ice.
Don't ask me why.
Be with me all the time.

translated by
Reza Mohseni Motlagh
Iran

NEGATIVE *TO BE* AND *TO HAVE* VERBS

TO BE

Present		Past	
I	am <u>not</u>	I	was <u>not</u>
he		he	
she	is <u>not</u>	she	was <u>not</u>
it		it	
you		you	
we	are <u>not</u>	we	were <u>not</u>
they		they	

TO HAVE

Present		Past	
I	<u>do not</u> have	I	<u>did not</u> have
he		he	
she	<u>does not</u> have	she	<u>did not</u> have
it		it	
you		you	
we	<u>do not</u> have	we	<u>did not</u> have
they		they	

The Seasons in My Country

Colombia has two seasons, winter and summer. It <u>DOES</u> <u>NOT</u> <u>HAVE</u> spring or autumn. In the winter, it rains frequently. People prefer to stay in their houses because the temperature is cool, but it <u>IS</u> <u>NOT</u> cold. The trees and the flowers grow, so you can see many colors: green, yellow, and red. Also you can smell delicious aromas. Everybody wears coats, scarves, and sweaters, and they drink hot coffee. In the summer, we <u>DO</u> <u>NOT</u> <u>HAVE</u> rain. The sun shines all day long. People like to go to parks and travel to other cities. The temperature is hot. For this reason, everybody wears light clothes. The trees and flowers grow, but they <u>ARE</u> <u>NOT</u> as fresh. I like summer because I can go to my farm with my family.

Maria Muñoz
Colombia

Exercise 2G

With a partner, read the following paragraphs. Then do the exercises that follow each paragraph.

I

The Seasons

Winter and summer are the seasons in Caracas, Venezuela. We do not have fall and spring. I prefer the winter because it is not too hot. In the winters, it rains a lot of the time. During the day, we have warmth, but we are not hot. On winter evenings we are cool. There are smells of the rivers and smells of the wet earth. The people in my hometown prefer winter because it is prettier. There are many flowers, and the green of the trees is very beautiful. The birds are very colorful, and they sing in the trees. The rain swells the rivers, and the rivers become brown. There are fresh fruits all the time.

Natalia Guerra
Venezuela

1. Underline the negative TO HAVE and TO BE verbs in the paragraph.
2. Circle the subjects in the negative TO HAVE and TO BE sentences.
3. Put parentheses ( ) around the THERE IS and THERE ARE sentences.
   Circle the subject in those sentences.
4. Why does Natalia prefer the winter in Venezuela?

II

The Seasons in My Hometown

Riyadh, the capital of Saudi Arabia, has four seasons. But the seasons are not the same length. Summer is four months long, and it is very hot. The schools are closed, and some people go to the sea to swim. Many people go to Taif City because it is not so hot in the mountains. I like the summer because it is not cold. At noon the air is very hot because the sun is shining. The spring and fall seasons in my country are only two months long. During these seasons, the air is very comfortable, and the trees are green. Some people travel to Medina because they want to visit the mosque. Other people travel outside the country because they do not have to work. The winter in Saudi Arabia is four months long. The weather is very cold. There is a lot of rain. Sometimes the weather is nice, but often it is not.

Hassan Hareeri
Saudi Arabia

1. (Circle) the negative TO HAVE and TO BE verbs in the paragraph.

2. Put parentheses ( ) around the subjects in the underlined sentences.

3. Which season does Hassan prefer? Why?

4. How many times does Hassan use the words *weather* and *seasons* in the paragraph? Why?

I long for autumn,
for the blue sky and drifting clouds.
Join me, oh! you yellow butterfly.
We'll sing and dance over that fragrant rose.

Van Tran
Vietnam

NEGATIVE REGULAR VERBS

	Present			Past	
I	do not	like*	I	did not	like*
he			he		go*
she	does not	come*	she	did not	feel*
it			it		see*
you			you		live*
we	do not	walk*	we	did not	walk*
they			they		drink*

*NOTE: The root form of the verb is used with the negative.

Exercise 2H

Individually (or with a partner), read the following paragraphs. Then do the exercises that follow each paragraph.

I

The Seasons in Somalia

In my city, and in my country, we have four seasons: summer, fall, winter, and spring. In the summer, every place is green, and the weather is warm and sunny. <u>Then everyone can be comfortable and happy</u>. Most people in Somalia like the summer because they do not feel cold, and they do not wear sweaters. In the fall, there is not any rain, and the weather is cold. <u>The leaves fall from the trees</u>. There is not any rain in the winter, either, but the weather is very hot. Finally, in the spring there is a lot of rain. <u>It is a season of great activity</u>. The farmers grow crops on their farms, and there is plenty of grass for the animals.

Mohamed Issa
Somalia

1. <u>Underline</u> the negative verbs (TO HAVE, TO BE, and PRESENT TENSE regular verbs) in the paragraph.

2. Put parentheses ( ) around the THERE IS and THERE ARE in the paragraph.

3. Make the <u>underlined</u> sentences negative.

4. How many times does Mohamed use the words *seasons* and *weather* in the paragraph? Why?

II

The Many Seasons in Turkey

If you go to Turkey, you can see three seasons at the same time. If you go to eastern Turkey, you will see that the weather is very cold. It is dark because the sun does not shine. There are not any leaves, and the roads are icy. People ski, but a lot of people also get sick because of the cold weather. <u>Snow covers the entire area</u>, and the people are not happy. But if you go to western Turkey, you will see spring. There are flowers, green grass, fruit, and sunshine. Western Turkey is a very good area. <u>A lot of people live there</u>. You will also see a lot of tourists. If you go to South Turkey, you will see the summer season. There is sunlight, and you will see flowers, fruits, green grass, and the sea. <u>A lot of men take sun baths because the sea is very cool</u>. There are many crops and products like fruits and vegetables for sale.

Mustafa Aytac
Turkey

1. <u>Underline</u> all the negative verbs in the paragraph.

2. <u>Underline</u> THERE IS and THERE ARE. (Circle) the subjects in those sentences.

3. Make the <u>underlined</u> sentences negative.

4. Would you go to eastern Turkey for a vacation?

III

Los Baños, Laguna in the Phillipines _____ me with its tropical
impress
climate. Green is everywhere: leaves, vines, bushes. I feel confused by the disorder,

and I _____ sometimes a little frightened by the abundant growth. <u>The</u>
be
<u>humidity and the heat of the country are also a great change from the dry plains of</u>

<u>my home in the United States.</u> <u>I have abandoned stockings and other unnecessary</u>

<u>clothing, and I usually dress in thongs, a cotton blouse, and a skirt.</u> The frequent

rain _____ from the cold, chilling rain of my hometown. Here, with 90 percent
differ
humidity in eighty-five degree air, there is no shock to the body when slightly more

concentrated moisture falls in the form of rain. My skin _____ from the even
benefit
moisture. It _____ and is even youthful. Now that I have adjusted to the
glow
climate in Los Baños, I _____ more comfortable.
feel

Ann Zimdahl
United States

1. Write the correct present tense form of the verbs in the blanks.
2. (Circle) the subject of each <u>underlined</u> sentence.
3. Write a title for this paragraph.
4. How does the rain in Los Baños differ from rain in Ann's hometown?

> In drowsy spring,
> I saw a cow standing in a
> field of drizzling rain.
>
> translated by
> *Mari Kanada*
> Japan

Writing Assignment

Write a paragraph about the seasons in your hometown. First, answer some of the questions below. Then, use the chart below to help plan your paragraph.

- How many seasons do you have in your hometown?

- What do you remember about each season?

- Which season is your favorite season? Why?

- Which season do you dislike? Why?

SEASONS

Adjectives	What do you see? hear? smell?
hot	_____
warm	_____
cold	_____
cool	_____
humid	_____
dry	_____
rainy	_____
windy	_____
snow	_____
ice	_____
green	_____

Interview

Ask a person NOT in your class to describe the seasons in his or her hometown. Ask some of the questions from the writing assignment above. Then write the answers in a paragraph. Use correct subject pronouns. Make sure each verb agrees with its subject. Use the chart below to indicate the differences in temperature between Fahrenheit and centigrade. Use sentences like:

- In the winter, the temperature ranges from _____ degrees C. (_____ degrees Fahrenheit) to _____ degrees C. (_____ Fahrenheit).

• In the summer, the temperature reaches _____ degrees C. (_____ degrees Fahrenheit) to _____ degrees C. (_____ Fahrenheit).

TEMPERATURE CONVERSION

C°	−40	−20	0	20	40	60	80	100	120	140	160	180	200	220	240	260
F°	−40 −20	0	20	40	60	80	100	120	140	160	180	200	220	240	260	280	300	320	340	360	380	400	420	440	460	480	500

HAIKU

Haiku: a Japanese poem <u>about nature</u> that has 17 syllables in a specific pattern:

line 1 = 5 syllables
line 2 = 7 syllables
line 3 = 5 syllables

Winter

1   2 3   4   5
Warmth, already gone   (5 syllables)

1   2   3   4   5   6   7
The cold has entered the town   (7 syllables)

1   2   3   4   5
Put your sweater on!   (5 syllables)

Said Pirnazar
Iran

Exercise 2I

Read the following haiku written by students. Count the syllables. Some of the haiku are not exactly the correct number of syllables.

Spring

Spring breeze comes to wake   _____ syllables
trees up, to begin new life   _____ syllables
after winter's sleep.   _____ syllables

Aziz Goharani
Iran

Summer

Nice smelling weather	_____ syllables
bright flowers bloom everywhere	_____ syllables
waiting for their end.	_____ syllables

Ziya Bozer
Turkey

Autumn

Sounds of ruffling leaves	_____ syllables
and the crispy air we breathe	_____ syllables
is the autumn breeze.	_____ syllables

Boyle Gaffar
Indonesia

Winter

Little pussy cat	_____ syllables
crouched in the dark corner:	_____ syllables
a soft woolen ball.	_____ syllables

Wai Ming Li
Hong Kong

Snow

It came from the sky	_____ syllables
like falling gleaming stars	_____ syllables
dressing the earth in white.	_____ syllables

Jose Viani
Venezuela

Evening

Far out in the west	_____ syllables
as the big red bulb drops,	_____ syllables
the silent world rests.	_____ syllables

Wai Ming Li
Hong Kong

Writing Assignment

Think about the seasons in your country. Then write a haiku about one of the seasons. Count the syllables. Try to follow the correct form of the poem.

Then share your haiku with several classmates in a small group. As you read your classmates' poems

- Count the number of syllables in each line, and write them at the end of the line.
- Make one suggestion for a word change that might help the author of the poem.
- At the end of each haiku, write one sentence about why you liked the poem.
- Discuss with your group the haiku you liked best. Why did you like it?

Other Writing Topics

- My Present Hometown
- My Favorite Room in My Present Home
- How I Feel When It Rains (or Snows)
- The Seasons in Another Part of My Country
- The Seasons in My Present Town

Writing Projects

Individual Booklets: Use the paragraph(s) you have written to begin a booklet about your hometown and about your home. Then write several more paragraphs about your hometown and your home. Illustrate the booklet with drawings and/or photographs. Use some of the titles below:

- My Friend's House
- My School
- Shops in My Hometown
- A Park in My Hometown
- My Favorite Place in My Hometown
- The Most Beautiful Building in My Hometown
- My Favorite Season in My Hometown

Use photographs of your hometown and your home to make your booklet more interesting. Make a colorful cover for your booklet. Display the booklet in your classroom, and invite other students from other classes to your classroom to see the booklets. Make copies of the booklets for all the members of the class. Or visit a local middle school or junior high school, speak to a class of U.S. students, and lend the booklets to the class so that they can learn more about your hometowns.

Group Project: Each student should write several haiku. Gather the haiku into a booklet. Decorate the pages and the cover of the booklet with small drawings and/or photographs of nature and the seasons.

3

Country

My Country's Flag

The Colombian flag's colors are yellow, blue, and red. These three colors are placed in horizontal bars, and the yellow stripe is double the size of the blue and red stripes. That is, the yellow bar is equal to both the red and the blue bars. The color yellow means the wealth of our soil; the gold mineral represents this wealth, and the yellow stripe is placed at the top of the flag. The middle bar is blue. It means the two oceans, the Atlantic and the Pacific, that border our territory. The last color, red, means the blood that was lost by our patriots to obtain liberty from Spain. This flag is similar to the flags of Ecuador and Venezuela because originally these three countries were united under the name of Gran Colombia (Great Colombia).

Danilo Valencia
Colombia

PREPOSITIONS OF PLACE

Prepositions of Place: WHERE?

in front ot

behind

in, inside of

on

under

over, above

beside

between

My country, you have my heart and my love.
My country, you must stay free,
And I depend on my God.

translated by
Tarik A. Tawfic
Egypt

PREPOSITIONAL PHRASES

PHRASE: a group of words that does NOT have a subject and/or does NOT have a verb.

Prepositional Phrase:

PREPOSITION + ARTICLE (a, an, the) + (adjective) + NOUN

Sample Prepositional Phrases of Place

The stars are (*in* **the corner**).
The stripes are (*on* **the white part**).
The eagle appears (*beside* **the circle**).
The moon is (*under* **the stripe**).
The star is (*between* **the red stripe and the white stripe**).
The five points (*on* **the star**) represent five countries.
The triangle is (*beside* **the circle**).
The moon is (*above* **the stars**).

Other Important Prepositions

The red color represents the blood (*of* **the people**).
Blue represents peace (*with* **all the people**) (*of* **the world**).
Our flag was designed (*by* **the patriots**) (*in* **our country**).
Green stands (*for* **the prosperity**) (*in* **our country**).
We carry our flag (*to* **our school**).

Indonesia's Flag

We Indonesians call our flag Merah-Pusih. *Merah* means "red," and *pusih* means "white." Our flag is rectangular. The width is two-thirds (*of* **the length**). It consists (*of* **two equal parts**), divided horizontally (*in* **the middle**). The color (*of* **the top part**) is red, and the bottom part is white. Red represents courage, and white means peace. Historically, the meaning *(of the flag)* is that Indonesians are brave. They also seek peace among themselves and *(with other countries) (in the world)*. *(On a special day)*, like Independence Day (August 17), we raise the flag *(on a pole) (in front) (of each house)*. We love and admire our flag very much. *(On Independence Day)*, the flag is raised while the independence song is played *(by a band)*. Usually the military bands play that song very well, so my love and pride *(of my country)* is aroused.

Istimawan Dipohusodo
Indonesia

Exercise 3A

Individually, or with a partner, read the following paragraphs. Then do the exercises that follow each paragraph.

I

The Flag of Somalia

Our country's flag looks like the sky. It is blue, and it has a white star with five points in the middle of the flag. The five-pointed star stands for the five parts of Somalia. Our flag was created by the freedom pioneers in my country in October 1954. Before that time, Somalia was an Italian and an English colony.

Abdinazak Mohamed Osman
Somalia

1. Put 8 prepositional phrases in parentheses ( ) .

2. Circle the noun (or pronoun) that follows each preposition.

3. What question could you ask Abdinazak about the underlined sentence?

4. Draw a picture of Somalia's flag here.

II

My Country's Flag

Every country has its own flag. Each flag _____ different colors and shapes which have different meanings. The flag of Vietnam does not look like any flag from any other country. My country's flag _____ simple. It _____ a yellow rectangle. There _____ three horizontal red stripes which go across from one end to the other end of the flag. The yellow color represents the color of my countrymen's skin. The three red lines represent three different areas in my country. These areas _____ North, Central, and South Vietnam. The red color represents the blood of my country. An overall meaning of my country's flag _____ that people with yellow skin live in three different areas which combine together as a country that _____ called Vietnam.

Minh Chu
Vietnam

1. Write the correct form of the verb TO BE and the verb TO HAVE in each blank.

2. Put parentheses ( ) around 10 prepositional phrases.

3. Circle the noun (or pronoun) in each prepositional phrase.

4. Draw the Vietnamese flag here.

War

> Blind purpose, blind faith.
> Blood of the young and innocent lives—
> Is it all in vain?
>
> Athur Javaid
> Pakistan

Interview

Ask a friend not from your country to describe his or her country's flag. As your friend describes the flag, draw the flag, but don't let your friend see what you draw. Then show your friend your drawing. Is it correct? What other information did your friend need to tell you?

Then, in a small group, share your drawing of your friend's flag. Discuss any problems that you and/or other group members had with your first drawings.

CLAUSES

CLAUSE: a group of words with a subject **(S)** and a verb **(V)**, and perhaps a complement **(C)**.

      (S)   **(V)**   **(C)**
1. My country's flag is (a rectangle).

      (S)   **(V)(C)**
2. Its color is (red).

   (S)(V)   **(C)**
3. It has (a green star in the middle).

My Country's Flag

     (S)   **(V)**   **(C)**   **(S)** **(V)(C)** **(S)(V)**   **(C)**
My country's flag is (a rectangle). The color is (red). It has (a green star in

         (S)   **(V)**   **(C)**   **(S)**
the middle). The red part of the flag stands (for blood). The people of Morocco

 (V)   **(C)**   **(S)**   **(V)**   **(C)**
fought (hard for independence). A lot of blood was spread (all over the country).

        (S)   **(V)**   **(C)**   **(S)**
The green star in the middle of the flag stands (for peace and prosperity). Morocco

 (V)   **(C)**   **(S)**   **(V)**   **(C)**
gained (independence from France in 1956). The people started (to work hard to

           (S)(V)   **(C)**   **(S)**
improve the social and economic situation). I am (proud of my country's flag). I

 (V)   **(C)**
know (the meaning of independence).

Abdelkader Assal
Morocco

Exercise 3B

In the paragraphs below, <u>underline</u> the subject of each clause and label it (S). Circle the verb in each clause and label it (V). Put parentheses ( ) around the complement in each clause and label it (C).

I

The Flag of the People's Republic of China

    The flag of the People's Republic of China (P.R.C.) is called the "Five Stars Red Flag." The flag is oblong. Its color is red. There are five yellow stars in the upper left corner of the flag. One of the stars is large. The other four are small. The large star is in the center. The others surround it. The red stands for socialism in the P.R.C. The yellow stars mean that the Chinese are a yellow people. The biggest star stands for the Communist party. The four smaller stars represent all the people in China. The red color also has another meaning. It stands for the blood of the great number of Chinese heroes. The founding of the P.R.C. is the result of innumerable people who died for their country.

Dong Aichu
China (P.R.C.)

II

The Flag of the United States

    The U.S. Flag is a rectangle. The long side of the rectangle contains thirteen stripes. The stripes alternate in colors of red and white. Each stripe stands for one of the original thirteen colonies that were established by British immigrants during the 17th century. In the upper left corner of the flag is a square of blue. On this blue square are fifty white stars. Each star represents one of the United States. The colors in the "red, white, and blue," as the flag is sometimes called, are symbolic. Red stands for the blood shed by U.S. citizens to achieve independence. White symbolizes the purity of those citizens. Blue represents their loyalty. In the U.S., June 14th is celebrated as Flag Day, the anniversary of the law in 1777 when Congress adopted the "Stars and Stripes" as the national flag. I am proud of how my flag represents the traits of hard work and honesty; it is a symbol of our tradition of freedom.

Keenon Hendon
United States

It takes both sunshine and rain to make a rainbow.

Cookie Sutter
United States

JOINING TWO CLAUSES

To Join Two Clauses: <u>S</u> + V (+ C) | , and | <u>S</u> + V (+ C)

Example:

      <u>Its color</u> is (red) | , and | <u>it</u> has (a green star in the middle). <u>The red part of the flag</u> is (for blood). <u>The people of Morocco</u> fought (hard for independence) | , and | <u>a lot of blood</u> was spread (all over the country). <u>The green star in the middle of my country's flag</u> stands (for peace and prosperity). <u>Morocco</u> gained (independence from France in 1956) | , and | <u>the people</u> started (to work hard to improve the social and economic situations). <u>I</u> am (proud of my country s flag) | , and | <u>I</u> know (the meaning of independence).

Abdelkader Assal
Morocco

Exercise 3C

With a partner, read the following paragraphs. <u>Underline</u> the subject of each clause. (Circle) the verb in each clause. Put a box around the | , and | that joins two clauses. Finally, try to draw each of the flags. What other information do you need to complete each flag?

I

Sri Lanka's National Flag

My country's flag is very beautiful. The background of the flag is yellow, and there is a picture of a lion with a sword on the flag. The people of my country have a relationship with the lion , and therefore special courage is with us. There are also two stripes of orange and green on our flag , and there are four *bo* leaves in the four corners. The four *bo* leaves are related to our religion , and they stand for peace and loving kindness. Most of the Sri Lankan people are Buddhists , and we respect the *bo* tree as a sacred tree. Our religious leader, the Lord Buddha, was enlightened under a *bo* tree.

B. D. Pathinyake
Sri Lanka

II

The Flag of Malaysia

Malaysia's flag looks like the U.S. flag. It has thirteen red and white horizontal stripes. The first stripe is red , and the second is white. This pattern continues until the thirteenth is red. A square of blue is in the upper left corner of the flag , and a yellow half-moon with one big star beside it is on the blue square. The thirteen stripes on the flag stand for the thirteen states in Malaysia. The red stripes represent the courage of the Malaysians , and the white stripes stand for the honesty of Malaysians. Malaysia is an Islamic country. Therefore, the moon and the star are the symbols of Islam as the first religion in Malaysia.

Nazari Mohamed
Malaysia

Drum

You beat a message,
Its joyful tempo a pledge:
Birth, wedding. A woe
its hoarse note:
Death, sorrow, foe.

translated by
Yenyou Bangole
Gabon

Writing Assignment

On a piece of paper, design and draw a flag for a new country. Use your imagination. Then, on another piece of paper, write a paragraph that describes that flag. Remember to use clear prepositional phrases. Answer some of the questions below:

• What colors are on the flag?

• What do those colors mean?

• What shapes are on the flag?

• What does each shape mean?

• Where is each color and each shape located on the flag?

Then exchange paragraphs with a partner (but don't show your partner your drawing!). As you read your partner's paragraphs, draw the flag described by your partner. Use ONLY the description written in the paragraph.

After that, exchange flag drawings. Are the drawings correct? What other information is needed to complete the drawings? Add that information to your paragraph.

Finally, in a small group, share your paragraph. Read several classmates' paragraphs. Which is the most interesting? Why?

Sunset

> Sunset glimmers on the beads of the curtains.
> Spring flowers bloom in the valley.
> The gardens along the river are filled with perfume.
> Smoke of cooking fires drifts across the slow barges.
> Sparrows hop in the branches.
> Whirling insects swarm in the air.
>
> > translated by
> > *Sin S. Chiu*
> > Hong Kong

Exercise 3D

Individually, or with a partner, read the following paragraphs. Then do the exercises that follow each paragraph.

I

The Flag of Korea

     If you want to learn about Korean philosophy, you should study our flag. <u>It holds the essence of orientalism.</u> Because our flag is complex, I will draw a picture of the flag. <u>First, the background of the flag is white.</u> <u>This color stands for the peace and the innocence of the Korean people.</u> Three black lines, some broken and some unbroken, are drawn diagonally at the four corners of the flag, and they represent the four seasons. The meaning of the three broken lines is spring. Four lines represent summer, five lines is fall, and six lines is winter. The continuous black lines are positive, and the broken lines are negative. A circle placed at the center of the flag represents the balance of space and nature. The circle is divided into two parts, and we call this curved line the *taeguk* mark. <u>The upper half is red, and it signifies positive, light, man, and heaven.</u> The lower half is blue, and it signifies negative, dark, woman, and the earth. Together, the positive and negative aspects of our flag signify the Korean people's love of balance and harmony.

Yong Ha Park
Korea

1. Put parentheses ( ) around 12 prepositional phrases.
2. (Circle) the noun (or pronoun) that follows each preposition.
3. Draw boxes around the ⌈ , and ⌉ joining the two clauses.
4. Make the <u>underlined</u> clauses negative.

II

The Flag of Taiwan, the Republic of China

There are three different colors in our country's flag: red, blue, and white.

It was designed by one of the national heroes of our country, H. T. Lu, seventy-

three years ago. On the surface of our country's flag, the white star in the upper right

corner _____ like the sun is just hanging in the center of the sky. The blue
      look

color _____ blue sky around all of us, and the red color _____ for blood
  represent   **stand**

which was shed when the revolution succeeded. In the left corner of my country's

flag, the white circle and twelve angles _____ the sun is shining and hanging
            mean

above our heads. Around this "sun," the blue color _____ the sky is very
          mean

beautiful and there _____ not any clouds in it. The rest of the flag, with its red
    be

color, means that the world is full of hope and happiness.

Wei-Fuu Yang
Taiwan (R.O.C.)

1. Write the correct present tense verbs in the blanks.
2. Put parentheses ( ) around 20 prepositional phrases.
3. Draw the Taiwanese flag.

4. What additional information do you need to draw the flag? What questions should you ask the author so that you can complete your drawing?

Another Spring

White birds over the grey river,
pink flowers on the green hills.
As I watch another spring go by,
I wonder when I shall return home again.

translated by
Maple Chan
Hong Kong

Exercise 3E

Read the paragraph that follows. It has many short clauses. Join some of the clauses with , and . *An asterisk (*) indicates where you should join the clauses. The first * has been completed for you. Remember: cross out the period (the full stop) at the end of the first sentence, and do NOT capitalize the first word of the second clause.*

The National Flag of Brazil

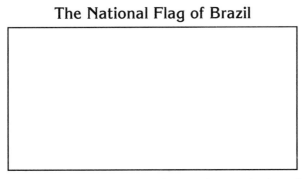

Brazil's flag is composed of four colors. It has four geometric figures * , and each one of them represents something important about Brazil's people or Brazil's history. Together they form a beautiful and harmonious combination. The flag is a green rectangle. * It represents Brazilian forests. Brazil is located mainly in the Amazonian region. * It is tropical and very green. There is a bright yellow stripe across the flag. * The yellow stands for the gold mined in Brazil. In the center of the flag, above the stripe, is a blue circle with stars. Blue is the color of Brazil's sky. * The white stars in the circle are a famous constellation. In the circle is the phrase, "Order and Progress." This motto encourages the Brazilian people to improve their way of life.

Jose Nilson Campos
Brazil

Each wrong step is a lost destiny, and each problem in life is a gained experience.

translated by
Semoa de Sousa
Sao Tomé, West Africa

MORE PREPOSITIONS

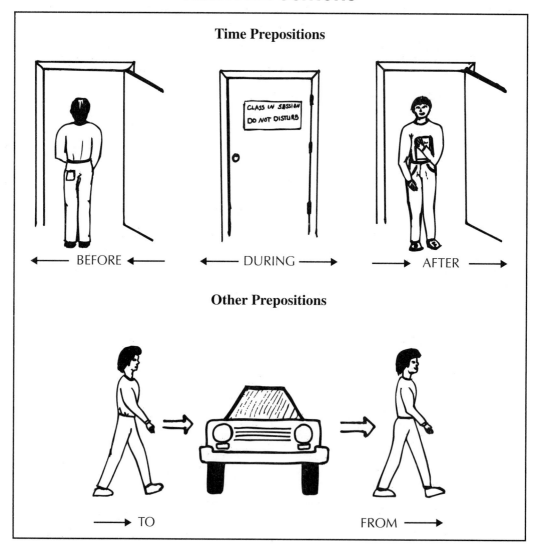

Time Prepositions

BEFORE   DURING   AFTER

Other Prepositions

TO   FROM

SAMPLE PREPOSITIONAL PHRASES

El Salvador was a Spanish colony *(before* **our independence**).

OR

(Before **our independence**), El Salvador was a Spanish colony.

We went home *(after* **the party**).

OR

(After **the party**), we went home.

Luis wore a costume *(during* **the celebration**).

OR

(During **the celebration**), Luis wore a costume.

The soldiers marched *(from* **the Capitol**) *(to* **the White House**).

The students *(from* **California**) came *(to* **the celebration**).

Indonesia's Celebration

Every year, *(on* **August 17th**), all Indonesians celebrate Independence Day. Indonesia gained independence *(on* **August 17, 1945**) *(after* **the Second World War**). *(After* **the war**), Indonesia began to develop the economics *(of* **the country**) and to educate its people. Although I am now *(in* **the United States**), I still celebrate my country's Independence Day. This year I invited my Indonesian friends and some American friends to come *(to* **my house**) *(for* **a party**). I prepared Indonesian food, and we celebrated all day.

Wishnoe Saleh Thaib
Indonesia

The rise and fall of a nation is the concern of every citizen.
Translated by
Hsiui Chen
Taiwan (R.O.C.)

Exercise 3F

Individually (or with a partner), read the following paragraphs. Then do the exercises that follow each paragraph.

I

An American Holiday

In the United States, it _____ customary for families to celebrate the American holiday of Thanksgiving with an enormous meal. Usually we _____ turkey, dressing (sometimes called stuffing), corn, sweet potatoes, cranberry sauce, mashed potatoes, rolls, and various other traditional dishes. For dessert, like most families, we serve different kinds of pie, most often apple or pumpkin. These traditional foods arose from the first Thanksgiving. Long ago, when the first pilgrims came to America, the Native Americans and the pilgrims got together, and they had a feast to give thanks for what they had. Today, as we _____ our Thanksgiving feasts with our families, we _____ the time to remember those people at the first Thanksgiving, and we _____ thanks for everything we have.

VERBS: eat   take   give   be   enjoy

Denise Linford
United States

1. Put parentheses ( ) around 8 prepositional phrases. ⬭Circle⬭ the noun (or pronoun) that follows each preposition.

2. Identify the subject (**S**) and the verb (**V**) in each <u>underlined</u> sentence.

3. Put a box around each ⬚ , and ⬚ that joins two clauses in this paragraph. Identify the subject (**S**) and the verb (**V**) in each of the clauses.

4. What questions can you ask Denise about her paragraph? How can she make her paragraph more interesting?

II

Carnival in Brazil

There is a big party in Brazil which is called "Carnival." It usually occurs

during the last part of February. For three days, people listen to the traditional music

that is called samba, and everybody _____ a good time. During the carnival,
have

people _____ happy. * Some of them wear funny dresses and _____
be   **paint**

their faces with many colors. On the second day, there _____ a beautiful
be

parade on the principal street of each city. People _____ costumes. * They
wear

dance. They throw candies to the other people. * They _____ confetti too.
throw
On the last day, there _____ another beautiful parade. People _____
be **go**
into the streets. They watch the "escola de samba." In this beautiful dance, the

people wear colorful costumes. After the "escola de samba," there _____
be
many parties. * People go to the parties in their costumes. In some cases, the men

_____ like women, or they put masks on their faces. In conclusion, at carnival
dress
time, everybody _____ a wonderful time.
have

Ademir Castro
Brazil

1. Write the correct present tense verbs in the blanks.
2. Put parentheses ( ) around 16 prepositional phrases. (Circle) the noun (or pronoun) that follows each preposition.
3. Underline the subject that follows each THERE IS or THERE ARE.
4. Join two clauses with | , and | where you see the asterisks (*).

> Patriotism is something to have,
> but it cannot be bought.
> If it could be gotten by money,
> even the stupid persons could have it.
> It is something very rare for a special person.
>
> translated by
> *Mahdi Ali*
> Somalia

SUBJECT-VERB AGREEMENT

Singular		Plural
Some**body**	IS	ARE
Every**body**	HAS	HAVE
No**body**	COOKS	COOK
Some**thing**	COMES	COME
Every**thing**	GOES	GO
Some**one**	WALKS	WALK
Every**one**	LISTENS	LISTEN

People

Exercise 3G

With a classmate, read the following paragraphs. Then do the exercises that follow each paragraph.

I

The Most Famous Holiday in My Country

One holiday in my country is Eid Aladha Almubarak. The reason for the holiday is to remember the time when the prophet Ibraham needed to kill his son Ishmail after his dream. Ibraham knew that his dream was from God because every prophet who dreamed anything about a person he loved very much knew the dream was an order from God. The morning after his dream, Ibraham told his son. * His son accepted it. When Ibraham began to kill his son, God sent a sheep to Ibraham to kill. The sheep was called "Adhia." Then Ibraham did not kill his son. From that day, most Muslims kill a sheep on the feast of Eid Aladha. On this day, the Muslims visit each other. * They cook a delicious meal with special food. The people give the children money to celebrate this day. * All of them are happy on this day.

Ameen Alawi
United Arab Emirates

1. Put parentheses ( ) around 8 prepositional phrases. Circle the noun (or the pronoun) that follows each preposition.

2. Identify the subject (**S**) and the verb (**V**) in each underlined sentence.

3. Join two clauses with | , and | where you see an asterisk (*).

4. What questions could you ask Ameen about this holiday?

II

Independence Day

        One of the biggest holidays in Cape Verde is Independence Day, on July 5. This day symbolizes freedom from colonial domination, exploitation, and slavery. The people endured colonialism for many years. * They struggled hard for a better education for their children. In other words, they were struggling to improve their situation. On Independence Day, the President gives a long speech. He talks about the founder of the political group who was killed. * He talks about himself when he was a prisoner. He announces the progress of the country. * He gives the plans that the government has for the future. The speech of the President is followed by a wonderful military parade. Also, there is a big popular party with the best musical group. Some people dance. The marchers exhibit the pictures of the people who died in the struggle for national liberation. When the Cape Verdian people became independent, they felt that they were really free and able to realize their dreams. Therefore, they enjoy this holiday every year.

Isaurinda Baptista
Cape Verde, West Africa

1. What is the main idea in this paragraph?

2. Identify the subject (**S**) and the (**V**) in each <u>underlined</u> sentence.

3. Join two clauses with ⌐ , and ⌐ where you see the asterisks (*).

4. How do people in Cape Verde celebrate Independence Day?

WRITING ASSIGNMENT

1. Write a paragraph about a famous holiday in your country. Answer some of the questions that are listed below.

   • What is the name of the holiday?

   • When is it?

   • Is it a religious holiday?

   • Is it a political holiday?

   • How do people celebrate the holiday?

   • What traditions are celebrated?

   • What is special about the celebration?

   • Do people wear costumes?

   • Do people prepare/eat special foods?

- Do people have special parties?

- What customs are celebrated?

- How long does it last?

2. Exchange paragraphs with a classmate.

   - Read the paragraph.

   - Ask your classmate any questions you have about your classmate's holiday.

   - Put parentheses ( ) around the prepositional phrases in your classmate's paragraph.

   - Draw a box around each ⌐, and⌐ that joins two clauses.

3. Rewrite your paragraph. Include new information that your partner asked about.

4. Share your paragraph with classmates in a small group. After you read several classmates' paragraphs, discuss the paragraph you like the most. Tell why you liked it.

   Some reasons might be:

   - Did you learn? What?

   - Was the paragraph amusing? How?

   - Was the detail interesting? In what ways?

   - Was it easy to read? Why?

> If you love something,
> leave it free.
> If it comes back to you, it's yours.
> But if it does not come back,
> it never was yours.
>
> translated by
> *Lorena Gabrie*
> Honduras

Exercise 3H

Read the following paragraphs. With a small group of classmates, do the exercises that follow each paragraph.

I

Chinese New Year

Chinese New Year is a public holiday in my home country, Malaysia. I

usually look forward to this day so that I can have a lot of fun like getting red-packets

from my elders and watching the lion dance. The red-packet _____ a
be

traditional Chinese gift from the elders to the young generations when they greet

them on New Year's Day. Everybody _____ happy to receive the red-packet
be

because it _____ good luck and a good start at the beginning of the new year.
represent

Inside the red-packet there is money. There is no specific sum. It can be fifty cents

or five dollars or ten dollars. Nobody _____ about the amount. Lion dancing
care

_____ another Chinese tradition for the new year. It _____ several
be   **need**

people. First, there are two people covered with the lion costume, and there are

others who play a big drum, cymbals, and other instruments. The "lion"

_____ down the street, and it _____ good luck. Therefore, a lot of
dance   **mean**

people _____ the lion back to their homes. When the lion _____ to a
invite   **come**

house, the family _____ a red-packet to a stick and raises the stick high in the
tie

air. The lion _____ the stick to get the red-packet.
climb

Man-Chiu Lu
Malaysia

1. Write the correct present tense verbs in the blanks.

2. Underline THERE IS/THERE ARE in the paragraph. ⟨Circle⟩ the subject that
   follows each THERE IS or THERE ARE.

3. Underline "everybody," "nobody," and "people" in the paragraph. Put brackets
   [ ] around the verb that follows each. Is it singular or plural?

4. Write two questions that you could ask Man-Chiu that would help you know
   more about Chinese New Year.

II

Celebrating the Japanese Rice Harvest

My favorite holiday _____ on the first Sunday of October. On that
                              be
day, we _____ the rice harvest. We _____ a big festival at our local
         celebrate   **have**
shrine on this holy day. There _____ many booths along the path to the shrine.
                                 be
People _____ crepes, ice cream, cookies, and cakes. My favorite cake
        buy
_____ waffle sweet. It _____ like a soft cloud shining in the sunset. In
 be   **be**
the early morning, my mother and sister _____ a special dinner. They
                                          prepare
_____ to great efforts in the kitchen. Generally, sushi _____ the main
 go   **be**
dish. When all my relatives _____ together, my home _____ festive.
                              come   **become**
My nieces and nephews _____ and _____ around. Because I
                       sing   **dance**
_____ to see children making happy noise, I do not mind at all.
 like
I _____ a very good time on this special day.
   have

Mitsuaki Uchida
Japan

1. Write the correct present tense verbs in the blanks. (Circle) the subject for
   each of those verbs.

2. What is the main idea of this paragraph?

3. Put parentheses ( ) around 10 prepositional phrases. Put a box around the
   noun (or the pronoun) that follows each preposition.

4. Rewrite this paragraph. Change "I," "we," and "my" to "she," "they," and
   "her." Be sure that each verb agrees with its subject.

III

Hajj

Hajj _____ the most popular holiday in my country. <u>It is an Islamic</u>
      be
<u>holiday, and it is in the last month of the year.</u> People _____ from far away to
                                                                  come

Medina and Mecca to visit these holy cities. Some people do not go to the holy cities because they do not have money or they are not well. The Quran says that these people can _____ to Mecca or Medina another year. At least one time during
go
their lives, they must go to Mecca. People who do not travel to holy cities fast on the feast of Hajj. On the second day, Muslims _____ together with friends.
gather
They cook meat, and the children wear new clothes.

Faizah Ahmad
Saudi Arabia

1. Write the correct present tense verbs in the blanks.
2. Underline the negative verbs in this paragraph.
3. Make the underlined sentences negative.
4. Write two questions that you could ask Faizah about Hajj.

If someone wants to live,
he will have to surmount every difficulty.
History shows that
all people who do not work seriously
have great problems in surviving.

translated by
Fakhreddine Karray
Tunisia

Interview

Interview a friend NOT in your class and NOT from your country about a holiday in his/her country. Ask some of the questions on pages 73–74. Then write the paragraph. Exchange paragraphs with a classmate.

A. Read the paragraph.

B. Put the prepositional phrases in parentheses ( ).

C. Draw a box around two clauses joined with ⎡ , and ⎤.

D. Ask two to four questions about the holiday that will help your partner make his or her paragraph more interesting.

Then answer your partner's questions about the holiday in your country. Rewrite your paragraph. Use your partner's questions to make your paragraph more interesting.

Finally, share your paragraph with some of your classmates in a small group. Read several classmates' paragraphs. Discuss the paragraph that interested you most with your classmates. Why did it interest you?

Exercise 3H

With a small group of classmates, read the following paragraphs. Then do the exercises that follow each paragraph.

I

My Country

Japan consists of four large islands and more than 300 small islands. The largest island _____ Honshu. It is in the center. To the north _____ Hokkaido. * To the southwest are Shikoku and Kyushu. Tokyo _____ the capital of Japan. It _____ on the island of Honshu. Tokyo is a very big city. * It has many companies. About eight million people live in Tokyo. The most famous mountain in Japan is Mount Fujiyama. It _____ 12,388 feet high. From the top of Mount Fuji, one can see the city of Tokyo. Other large cities in Japan _____ Osaka, Sapporo, Yokohama, and Nagasaki. Each of these cities has famous shrines and historical places.

Akiko Kudo
Japan

1. Write the correct form of the verb TO BE in the blanks.

2. Join two clauses with , and , but or , so where you see the asterisk (*).

3. Put parentheses ( ) around five prepositional phrases.

4. Akiko has written statements about many things. However, almost every statement could begin a new, interesting paragraph. Here are some questions you could ask about the sentences:

- How large is Honshu?
- What are the largest cities on Honshu?
- What's the weather like on Honshu?
- How large are the large Honshu cities?
- How many people live on Honshu?
- What are the major industries there?
- Are there famous parks on Honshu?
- Are there other special places there?
- Where is Mount Fuji?

- Does it have a special shape?
- Why is it famous?
- Is Mount Fuji important culturally?
- What does the name mean?
- Do people climb Mount Fuji?

With your group, discuss what questions you could ask Akiko about other sentences in the paragraph.

II

The Climate and the Crops in Cambodia

CAMBODIA (Kampuchea)

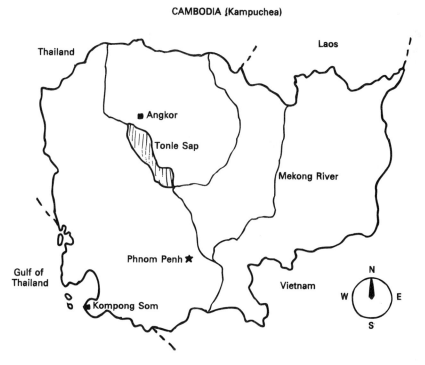

Cambodia is a small country located in Southeast Asia. The land surface is flat. * Mountains surround its borders. The mountains have jungles which are full of plants and wild animals. In Cambodia there are two types of weather: hot and rainy. During the winter, the heavy rainfall and the warm temperatures are just right for growing rice. * Most people in Cambodia work on their farms during the whole season. They take care of the plants until the summer. During the hot weather, the people collect their rice from the fields. * They put it in the supply house. If they make a lot of rice, they keep only enough for their family. They sell the rest to the government because they need the money to buy some things. However, people in Cambodia also grow vegetables, tobacco, or anything they need. In the summer, the farm work is finished. * Some people visit their relatives for a few months. I like the hot weather in my country. * I also like the rain that makes everything grow.

Farid Soeu
Cambodia

1. Join two clauses with | , and | | , but | or | , so | where you see the asterisk (*).
2. (Circle) the subject (S) and put a box around the verb | V | in the underlined sentences.
3. How does Farid's map help you to understand his paragraph?
4. Write two questions that you could ask Farid about Cambodia. Then share your questions with your group. Use the questions to discuss, with your classmates, what other paragraphs Farid could write about his country.

III

The Geography of Honduras

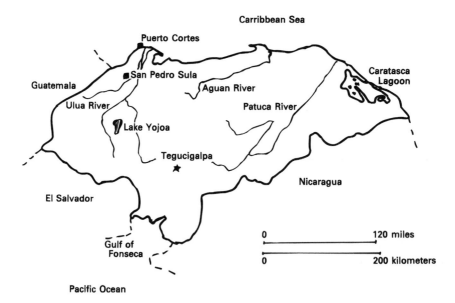

HONDURAS

Honduras is a small country with many interesting geographical areas and a tropical climate. The population in Honduras is about 4 million inhabitants. * It has a total area of 43,277 square miles. It has many rivers and mountains. The most important and largest rivers are the Ulve and the Patuca. The highest and the most important mountains are the Cordillera de Merendon in the west and the Cordillera de Agalta in the northeast of the country. The seasons are not marked. For example, Honduras does not get snow at all. * The lowest temperature ever recorded was zero degrees F. Almost all year it is summer on the coast and spring in the rest of the country. <u>In the center of Honduras, the winds blow often.</u> * <u>The temperature changes very often.</u> There is only one large lake in Honduras. It is called *Lago de Yojoa.* * It is located in the west, between two important cities, Santa Barbara and Siguatepeque. In addition, Honduras has many forests. Honduras is a beautiful country. * I am happy that it is my country.

Olga Handal
Honduras

1. Join two clauses with | , and | | , but | or | , so | where you see the asterisk (*).
2. Make the <u>underlined</u> clauses negative.
3. How does Olga's map help you understand her paragraph?
4. What questions could you ask Olga about her country? With your group, discuss what other paragraphs Olga could write about her country.

Song of Five Friends

How many friends have I? Count them:
Water and stone, pine and bamboo,
the rising moon on the east mountain.
I welcome the moon—it too is my friend.
What need is there, I say,
to have more friends than five?

translated by
Chul Lee
Korea

Writing Assignment

1. Make a map of your country and the countries or seas surrounding it. Put the major cities, major rivers and lakes, and major mountains and deserts on the map. Then write THREE paragraphs about your country. Use some of the topics below.

   • The Geography of My Country
   • The Rivers of My Country

- A Famous Desert in My Country

- The Most Famous Mountain in My Country

- The Largest City in My Country

- The Political System in My Country

- An Important Crop in My Country

- A Place Tourists Visit in My Country

- A City for Vacationing in My Country

- _____

2. To plan your paragraph, make a chart like the two on these pages:

AN IMPORTANT CROP IN MY COUNTRY

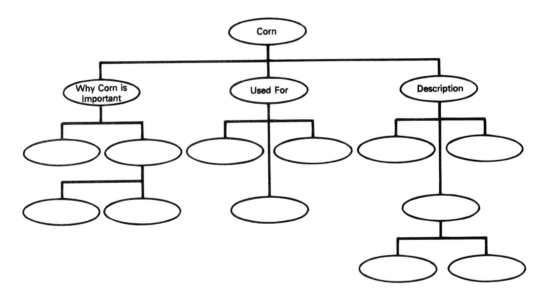

MAJOR RIVERS IN MY COUNTRY

- Rivers in My Country
  - River A
    - Waterfalls
    - Runs Through the Mountains
    - Exciting
      - Dangerous
      - Fast-Moving
  - River B
    - Transportation
      - For Crops
      - For People
      - For Lumber
    - Length
      - 400 Kilometers
      - Goes to the Sea
  - River C
    - Description
      - Warm Water
      - Beautiful
    - Recreation
      - Boating
      - Swimming

3. Exchange papers with a partner. As you read your partner's paragraphs, do the following:

   A. In the first paragraph, <u>underline</u> the connectors. Put parentheses ( ) around the prepositional phrases.

   B. In the second paragraph, put a box around each ⟨ , and ⟩ ⟨ , but ⟩ or ⟨ , so ⟩ that joins two clauses.

   C. In the third paragraph, put an asterisk (*) between 2 clauses that could be joined by *and, but,* or *so.*

   D. Ask your partner one question about each paragraph so that your partner can make her or his paragraph more complete and interesting.

4. Reread <u>your</u> paragraphs. How can you make your paragraphs more interesting? Use your own ideas and your classmate's questions to revise your paragraphs. Also, decide whether or not you want to join clauses in paragraph III where your partner put an asterisk (*). Next, rewrite your paragraphs.

5. Share your paragraphs with a small group of classmates. Read the paragraphs of two to four classmates. At the end of each of the student's paragraphs, write one sentence about what you liked about the paragraph, and ask one question that will help the author make his or her paragraph more interesting.

6. Reread your paragraph. Use the questions of your classmates to make your paragraphs more detailed and more interesting. Revise and then rewrite your paragraph.

Other Writing Topics

- The Largest City in My Country
- My Favorite Vacation Place in My Country
- A Famous Historical Place in My Country
- The Most Beautiful Place in My Country
- A Place Where Many Tourists Go in My Country
- A Place Where Tourists Do Not Go in My Country
- My Favorite Book
- My Favorite Sport
- What I Do on a Weekday in My Country
- What I Do on a Weekend Day in My Country

Writing Projects

Individual Projects:

1. Write several paragraphs about several different holidays in your country. Write paragraphs about some of the topics listed.

   • A Small Town in My Country

   • The Largest City in My Country

   • My Favorite Vacation Place in My Country

   • A Famous Historical Place in My Country

   • The Most Beautiful Place in My Country

   • A Place Where Many Tourists Go in My Country

   • A Place Where Tourists Do Not Go in My Country

   Make a booklet with the paragraphs about special places in your country. Include in the booklet maps and/or photographs. Give the booklet to a public school library to use with the students in that school.

2. Write several paragraphs about several different holidays in your country. Write paragraphs about some of the topics listed.

   • My Favorite Holiday

   • Traditional Dress for Women During _____ Holiday

   • Traditional Dress for Men During _____ Holiday

   • A Famous Person Who Is Honored by a Holiday in My Country

   • Preparing for _____ Holiday in My Country

   • A Special Holiday in My Hometown

   Make a booklet with the paragraphs about famous holidays in your country. Include in the booklet photographs or drawings of traditional dress and costume of those celebrations. Decorate the booklet with drawings or photographs of the celebrations. Give the booklet to a public school library to use with the students in that school.

Group Project: Make a booklet of flags of many countries of the world. Gather colorful pictures of flags of the countries of the students in class. You may include flags of other countries as well. Write paragraphs that describe the meanings of the flags. Present the booklet to a public school library to use with the students in that school.

4

Culture

Fathers and Mothers

A proverb in China says, "Fathers are outdoors, mothers are indoors." It means that fathers have to work hard for the support of the family, so they have to be outdoors—to work. And mothers are considered to be indoors—to do the housework, to take care of the children. But that does not mean the father has no responsibility in raising children. We Chinese think that child raising is the most important thing in a family, and mental health is an essential part of it. The children need to know gentleness as well as aggressive feelings. So it is the responsibility of mothers to teach the children what a gentle feeling is, a peaceful feeling rather than an aggressive one. The responsibility of fathers is the opposite. Fathers have to advise the children when there comes a hard time. He teaches them how to fight back with aggressive feelings. In recent years the structure of our society has changed a lot, but the roles in child raising are still unchanged.

Hung-chi Kuo
China (P.R.C.)

> If you have knowledge, you will be able,
> and from knowledge the old person's heart becomes young
>
> translated by
Medhi Medawi
Iran

ARTICLES

INDEFINITE		DEFINITE	
a(n) + noun		**the + noun**	
Singular	**Plural**	**Singular**	**Plural**
a mother	(X) mother**s**	**the** mother	**the** mother**s**
a child	(X) children	**the** child	**the** children
an infant	(X) infant**s**	**the** infant	**the** infant**s**

a(n) + adjective + noun

Singular	Plural
a successful father	(X) successful father**s**
an important job	(X) important job**s**

the + adjective + noun

Singular	Plural
the successful father	**the** successful father**s**
the important job	**the** important job**s**

Some Exceptions

The father brings the money (X) *home.*
The children go to (X) *school.*

NOTE: The correct use of articles in English is very complicated, especially for speakers of languages that do not use articles. However, about 80% of article use is easy to learn. For the remaining 20%, ask a native English speaker for help. That's the fastest and most accurate strategy.

The Responsibilities of Raising Children

<u>The</u> father is <u>an</u> important part of the family. First of all, he has to work outside the house to support his family. When he returns (X) home, he helps the children with their homework, and he asks what they did in (X) school. On the weekends, he wakes up early, and he takes his children to <u>a</u> movie or to <u>the</u> park. Then he takes them to <u>the</u> store to buy them what they need, like books, clothes, and toys. <u>The</u> father also teaches his children to behave well and to respect other people. He shows them how to be polite, how to talk in <u>a</u> clear voice, and how to pay attention to their teachers. Finally, <u>the</u> father helps his children to be confident and to fight for their rights, even in <u>the</u> worst situations. <u>The</u> father in Libya works more for his children than for himself.

Khadja Al Walda
Libya

An unkind teacher is better than a kind father.

translated by
Adel Salamah
Saudi Arabia

Exercise 4A

Read the following paragraphs. Then do the exercises that follow each paragraph.

I

Raising Children in France

<u>European culture is male-dominated</u>. This phenomenon appears everywhere, especially in child-raising. <u>The father and mother have two different purposes</u>. <u>The father is the symbol of authority and morality, but the mother gives the children affection and creates a sweet environment without hurt or shock</u>. Usually the place of the mother is more important because the children are in contact with her more than with their father. The father is often gone because his duty is to earn the money which is necessary to raise the children. <u>I think that the mother and father are both important</u>. They approach their children with different feelings and objectives. We cannot say that one is more important for the children. In France, child-raising is based on the complementary experiences given by both parents.

Jacques Ferraré
France

1. (Circle) 12 articles in the paragraph. <u>Underline</u> the nouns (or the adjectives and the nouns) that follow each article.

2. Put 8 prepositional phrases in parentheses ( ).

3. Make the <u>underlined</u> sentences negative.

4. What are the responsibilities of the mother in France? What are the responsibilities of the father?

II

A Mother's Responsibility

<u>A mother in the United States has many responsibilities in raising children</u>. Of course, both she and the father are obligated to provide the three fundamental needs of living: food, shelter, and clothing. <u>The mother is also primarily responsible for the physical health of the children</u>, and she needs to encourage all of their "firsts," such as their first words and first steps. Once the children enter school, the mother needs to prepare them for all that will come. She should, for example, praise each success the children encounter in life, and when they fail, the mother should provide hope and encouragement for the future. Even as the children start their own lives, the mother will provide support and love. Throughout her children's lives, <u>the mother will nurture them</u>.

Melissa F. Rousselle
United States

1. (Circle) 12 articles in the paragraph. (Circle) the nouns (or the adjectives and the nouns) that follow each article.

2. Put 5 prepositional phrases in parentheses ( ).

3. Make the <u>underlined</u> sentences negative.

4. How are the responsibilities of mothers in the U.S. similar to mothers' responsibilities in your country? How are they different?

III

The Roles of Mothers and Fathers

In my country, the roles of the mother and father in raising

children _____ similar. Both parents _____ education, medical care,
        be   **give**

protection, love, and the material things that their children need. But the difference

_____ that the mother _____ the responsibility of taking care of the
    be   **have**
child most of the time at (**X**) home. If a mother _____ , she _____ a
                                      work   **need**
person to help her at **X** home. The mother _____ food, _____ clothes,
                                       make   **wash**
_____ the baby, _____ the rules, and _____ the behavior of the
  bathe   **teach**   **manage**
children. On the other hand, the father _____ and _____ the money (**X**)
                                       work   **bring**
home. He _____ his wife with the children at night, but not much. He is
             help
interested in his children, but he _____ no time during the week. On the
                               have
weekends, when he _____ at home, he _____ with his children.
               be   **play**

Aleida Perez de Chavez
Venezuela

1. Write the correct form of the present tense verbs in the blanks.
2. (Circle) 18 articles in the paragraph. <u>Underline</u> the noun (or the adjective and the noun) that follows each article.
3. Put parentheses ( ) around 13 prepositional phrases.
4. How is child raising in Venezuela similar to child raising in France (paragraph I)?

Interview 👥 *and Writing Assignment*

    Ask a friend NOT in your class to describe the responsibilities that mothers and fathers in his or her country have in raising children. Ask your friend some of the questions below to learn more about raising children in that country. Then write a paragraph about your friend's information.

Which parent

- teaches the child to speak?
- bathes the child?
- punishes the child?
- takes the child to school?

- takes the child to the doctor?
- takes the child shopping?

Is one parent more responsible

- for taking care of the very young child?
- for taking care of the older child?
- for raising the sons?
- for raising the daughters?

1. Exchange paragraphs with a classmate.
    - Read your partner's paragraph.
    - (Circle) the articles in the paragraph.
    - Put parentheses ( ) around the prepositional phrases.
    - Draw a box around the | , and | that joins two clauses.
    - Ask your partner one to three questions about details that will make the paragraph more interesting.

2. Reread your paragraph. Look again at the information in the paragraph. Answer your partner's questions about your paragraph. You may have to interview your friend again in order to answer the questions.

3. Now, rewrite your paragraph. Remember to use the additional information that will make your paragraph more interesting.

4. Finally, share your new paragraph with several classmates in a small group. After you read two to four paragraphs, discuss with your group the most interesting paragraph you read. Why did you like it?

Virtue leads to happiness, and vice leads to misery.

                                                        translated by
                                                        Kyu-Yong Lee
                                                        Korea

CONNECTORS

Additional Information	Explanatory Information	Contrasting Information
also	that is,	but
in addition,	for example,	however,
and	in fact,	
besides X,	for instance,	
in addition to X,		

Pakistani Fathers

The responsibilities of a father start when a child is about five years old. The father takes the child to a proper school, <u>AND</u> he pays the school expenses. He <u>ALSO</u> checks the physical as well as the mental progress of his child, <u>AND</u> he guides the child. <u>IN ADDITION</u>, the father tells his child about the relationships with other family members. Whenever the father gets some time, he takes the child to famous places. On the way, he tells the stories of his ancestors <u>AND</u> thus tries to produce a personality which is according to family traditions. The children will learn from their father, <u>AND</u> they will love him too.

M. Hanif
Pakistan

Exercise 4B

Read the following paragraphs. Then do the exercises that follow each paragraph.

I

_____

The responsibilities mothers have in my country _____ teaching their
  be
children morals, behavior, and discipline. When they _____ very young,
  be
children do not know what is bad and what is good. The mother _____ the
  be
person who can tell her children about the bad things and the good things. For

instance, when the mother goes to the grocery store, the child might take something.

The mother must tell the child that if he _____ anything, he must pay for it. If
                                              take
the mother _____ her child telling jokes about an old or a handicapped person,
              see
she must scold him. She will also teach her child to respect and help other people,

and she will teach him to wash his face and to make his bed every day. A good

mother can make a good child by taking the proper responsibility for his behavior.

Parvin Sultana
Bangladesh

1. Write the correct forms of the present tense verbs in the blanks.
2. <u>Underline</u> 3 connectors in the paragraph.
3. (Circle) 10 articles in the paragraph.
4. Write a title for this paragraph.

II

Fathers in Jordan

Fathers in my country do hard work for their children. First, fathers take

care of their children. For example, they _____ them clothes, toys, and food.
                                               buy
In addition, if a child feels some pain, the father _____ him to the doctor and
                                                        carry
_____ medicine for him. Fathers also _____ their children the
  buy   **teach**
importance of education.   In fact.   this _____ when the child
                                                  begin
_____ elementary school.   Second, fathers _____ advice to their
  enter   **give**
children during their teenage years. For example, fathers _____ their children
                                                               tell
how to choose friends and how not to be friends with lazy, careless, drunken,

nonreligious students. Fathers also teach their children the importance of following

Islamic rules. A father _____ his son to become educated, to be innocent and
                            encourage

active, and to worship Allah. He _____ his son how to serve Islam by using
teach
his talents and by sacrificing for his country.

Hasan Al-Mohamed
Jordan

1. Write the correct present tense verbs in the blanks.
2. <u>Underline</u> 6 connectors in the paragraph.
3. What do you remember about Hasan's paragraph?
4. What questions could you ask Hasan about this paragraph?

Writing Assignment

1. Write two paragraphs. In the first paragraph, write about the responsibilities that
mothers in your country have in raising children. In the second paragraph, write
about the responsibilities fathers in your country have in raising children. Use
appropriate connectors in the paragraphs. Use the chart below to help plan your
paragraph.

Responsibilities of the Mother in My Country

taking care of the child   For example, _____

teaching the child   For example, _____

_____   For instance, _____

     For example, _____

     In addition, _____

     Also, _____

Responsibilities of the Father in My Country

supporting the child   For example, _____

teaching the child   For instance, _____

_____   For example, _____

     In addition, _____

     Also, _____

---

2. Exchange paragraphs with a classmate. Read both paragraphs.

    A. In the first paragraph (about mothers' responsibilities), <u>underline</u> the connectors. Then ⟨circle⟩ the articles.

    B. In the second paragraph (about fathers' responsibilities), <u>underline</u> the prepositional phrases. Then ⟨circle⟩ the noun that follows each preposition.

    C. Ask your classmate two questions to learn more about the responsibilities of parents in his or her country.

3. Reread your paragraphs. How can you make your paragraphs more interesting? Use your own ideas and your classmate's ideas to revise your paragraphs. Next, rewrite your paragraphs.

4. Share your paragraphs with a small group of classmates. Read the paragraphs of two to four classmates. At the end of each of the student's paragraphs, write one sentence about what you liked about the paragraph, and one questions that will help the author make his or her paragraph more interesting.

5. Reread your paragraphs. Use the questions of your classmates to make your paragraphs more detailed and more interesting. Revise and then rewrite your paragraphs.

> God takes his time, but he never forgets.
>
> translated by
> *Douglas Chang*
> Ecuador

CHRONOLOGICAL (TIME) CONNECTORS

First,…	Before X,…	Then,…
Second,…	After X,…	Next,…
Third,…	During X, …	Finally,…
	Afterwards,…	After that,…

How to Cook One of My Favorite Foods

I'm going to write about how to cook chicken gizzards. <u>FIRST</u>, you have to wash and cut the chicken gizzards. <u>SECOND</u>, you have to put them into the pot. Do not add water because the chicken gizzards have their own water. <u>THEN</u> cook the gizzards. <u>AFTER</u> the liquid decreases, put one glass of hot water into the pot. You have to repeat that twice. <u>THIRD</u>, when the chicken gizzards are soft, you need to cut an onion and to fry it. <u>THEN</u> you put the fried onion in the pot with the chicken gizzards. <u>AFTER</u> <u>THAT</u>, add salt and pepper. <u>FINALLY</u>, you have one plate of excellent chicken gizzards.

Maria M. Lopez
Colombia

> Eating is more
> important than looking at
> pretty blossoms.
>
> translated by
> *Mari Kaneda*
> Japan

Exercise 4C

With a small group of classmates, read the following paragraphs. Then do the exercises that follow each paragraph.

I

Cooking Spaghetti

It is easy to learn how to make spaghetti. First, I <u>put</u> some water, salt, and oil in a pan. Then I <u>put</u> the pan on the stove for about 15 minutes. After this, I <u>put</u> the spaghetti into the pan for ten minutes. Then I <u>take</u> the pan off the stove. After that, I <u>put</u> tomato juice, oil, salt, and meat in another pan. I <u>cook</u> these ingredients on the stove for half an hour. After a while, I <u>take</u> the spaghetti out of the pan, and I <u>serve</u> it. I <u>put</u> the sauce on top of the spaghetti, and I <u>serve</u> it with cheese.

Mariam Peaspan
Italy

1. Rewrite the paragraph. Substitute "she" for "I." Remember to change the <u>underlined</u> present tense verbs to agree with the new subject:

I <u>put</u> ⟶ she <u>puts</u>

2. Put parentheses ( ) around the prepositional phrases. (Circle) the noun that follows each preposition.

3. Underline 6 chronological (time) connectors.

4. Many readers of this paragraph could not make spaghetti without more information. Discuss with your group how Mariam might revise her paragraph. What questions could you ask her?

II

How to Make Rice

I make rice almost every day. First, I put some water in a pot. * Then I put the pot on the fire. When it becomes hot, I add some salt to it. Second, I put rice in the pot that contains the water. Third, I add some butter. * I cook the rice over a medium fire for about 15 minutes. Finally, the rice is ready. * I serve it to my guests.

Ahmed Badahdah
Saudi Arabia

1. Rewrite Ahmed's paragraph. Change each "I" to "he." Change the underlined present tense verbs to agree with the new subject.

2. Join two clauses with , and where you see the asterisk (*).

3. Underline 5 chronological connectors.

4. Could you make rice by following Ahmed's directions? With your group, discuss how Ahmed could revise this paragraph. What questions could you ask him?

> Where there is sugar, there is an ant.
>
> translated by
> *Sri Peni*
> Indonesia

Writing Assignment

1. Read the recipe below. Then write a paragraph that tells a friend how to make that recipe. Use chronological connectors. The meanings of the abbreviations are:

   T. = tablespoon   **t.** = teaspoon

SCRAMBLED EGGS

1–2 T. butter 3 eggs	1. Melt in a pan over low heat
	2. Beat with a fork until the eggs are thoroughly mixed

Add and mix into the eggs: | **Optional additions:**

1/4 t. salt

1/8 t. paprika

2 T. milk or cream

grated cheese

chopped tomatoes

chopped onion

sauteed mushrooms

Pour the mixture into the pan. Cook slowly, turning the eggs with a spoon until the mixture thickens. Makes two servings.

2. Show your paragraph about scrambled eggs to a friend who is NOT in your class. Does your friend understand each step? Does he or she have questions that must be answered to complete the recipe?

3. Revise your paragraph by adding any necessary information to your paragraph. Then rewrite your paragraph.

A bird in the hand is better than ten on the tree.

translated by
Said Pirnazar
Iran

IMPERATIVES (GIVING DIRECTIONS)

(you +)   **Root Form of the Verb + Complement.**

Mix* the ingredients.

Bake* the cake.

Be* careful.

Go* to the oven.

Serve* the guests.

Sit* down.

*NOTE: The root form of the verb is used in the imperative.

How to Bake a Cake

I like cakes, and they are easy to bake. First, <u>READ</u> the recipe carefully. Then <u>GATHER</u> the ingredients and <u>TURN</u> on the oven to 350 degrees F. After that, <u>MIX</u> the sugar with the butter. <u>ADD</u> the flour and <u>CONTINUE</u> mixing for fifteen minutes. Next, <u>TURN</u> off the beater and <u>POUR</u> the mixture into a cake pan. After that, <u>PUT</u> the cake in the oven. Finally, after half-an-hour, <u>CHECK</u> to see if the cake is ready, and <u>TAKE</u> the cake out of the oven.

Yusmary Espinoza
Venezuela

Exercise 4D

With a partner, read the following paragraphs. Then do the exercises that follow each paragraph.

I

Kabsa

It is not difficult to make Kabsa. First, you need a pot, water, rice, onion, tomato, and some spices. To cook the kabsa, fry the onion for two minutes. <u>Then add the tomato with some salt and spices</u>. After that, pour in some water. The amount of water should be double the rice. For example, if you are going to use one cup of rice, use two cups of water. <u>After a while, add the rice and put the lid on the pot for thirty minutes</u>. After that, you will find that a delicious dish is waiting for you to enjoy.

Fares El-Ja
Kuwait

1. <u>Underline</u> 6 imperatives in the paragraph.
2. Circle 6 chronological connectors.
3. Make the <u>underlined</u> sentences negative.
4. Could you make Kabsa by following Fares' instructions? How might the author revise this paragraph? What questions could you ask Fares about his recipe?

II

Making Caipiriuha

Follow these steps, and you will have a typical Brazilian drink called Caipiriuha. First, buy the ingredients: cachac'a (a Brazilian alcoholic beverage made out of sugar cane), lemon, and sugar. If you cannot find cachac'a, vodka will do. After that, start the mixing. Squeeze 4 lemons and mix them with 1/2 cup of water. Then put this mixture in a jar with two cups of cachac'a, and mix them very well. Finally, add some crushed ice. Then taste it. Modify the amount of each ingredient according to your taste. Before serving the drink, put a slice of lemon in each glass to make it more appealing. Serve Caipiriuha in large glasses, and enjoy it!

Marluce Albuquerque
Brazil

1. <u>Underline</u> 10 imperative verbs in the paragraph.
2. (Circle) 4 chronological connectors.
3. Put parentheses ( ) around 7 articles.
4. Could you make this recipe by following Marluce's instructions? What questions could you ask Marluce about her recipe? In what ways might she revise her paragraph?

> The person who has bread doesn't have teeth, and the person who has teeth doesn't have bread.
>
> translated by
> *Semoa de Sousa*
> Sao Tomé, West Africa

Writing Assignment

1. Write a paragraph about how to cook a food from your country. Answer some of the following questions.
   - What is the food?
   - What are the ingredients?
   - How much of each ingredient do you use?
   - What steps do you follow to cook the food?
     - First,…
     - Second,…
     - After that,…
   - How long does each step take?
   - How does the food smell?
   - How does the food taste?

2. Exchange paragraphs with a classmate. Read your partner's paragraph. Could you make that food? Ask your partner any necessary questions to complete the recipe.

3. Reread your paragraph. Read it aloud and listen to the paragraph. Then, using your own ideas (and your partner's questions), revise your paragraph to make it more complete and interesting.

4. Rewrite your paragraph. Then share your paragraph with a small group of classmates.

> Do not be either too soft, or you will be kneaded, or too hard, for you will be broken.
>
> translated by
> *Adel Salamah*
> Iran

Collaborative Writing Assignment

1. With a partner or a small group of classmates, look at the chart below that describes the kinds of international restaurants most liked by North Americans. Then write <u>one paragraph</u> (together) that describes the chart. Answer some of the questions listed.

   • What percentage of Americans like Italian food?

   • What percentage of Americans like Chinese food?

   • What percentage of Americans like the other kinds of food on the chart?

   • Why do Americans like these international foods?

   • What international foods do people in your country like? Why?

2. Use some of the following sentences to write your paragraph:

   According to the National Restaurant Association,…

   • more than _____ Americans like *X*.

   • many Americans also like *X*.

   • in addition, _____% of Americans like *X*.

   • some Americans, _____%, like *X*.

   • a few Americans, _____%, like *X*.

   I think Americans like international food because…

AMERICA'S FAVORITE RESTAURANTS

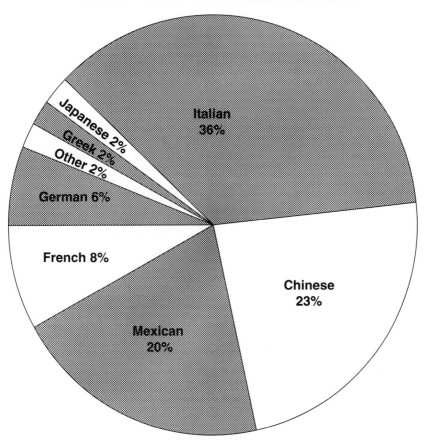

I love you O' my heartbeat.
I love you O' best love in my life.
Your love is my destination.
Your love is my hope.
Although life separated us,
You are close to me.

translated by
Hassan Hareeri
Saudi Arabia

JOINING CLAUSES
WITH CONNECTORS

Additional Information

S + V (+C) ⟨**, and**⟩ S + V (+C).

Contrasting Information

S + V (+ C) ⟨**, but**⟩ S + V (+ C).

Cause-effect Information

S + V(+ C) ⟨**, so**⟩ S + V (+ C).

NOTE: NEVER begin a line with a comma. Put the comma at the end of the previous line.

Wedding Customs in Iran

There are three phases that Iranians usually follow when a man and a woman get married. First, a man chooses a girl, and then he has to talk with his parents. If his parents are satisfied with the future bride, they arrange to meet the girl's parents. The man and his parents put on new clothing , AND they go to the girl's home. They discuss the marriage with the girl's parents , BUT the girl is not present. Afterwards, if the girl and her parents are pleased with the man, the girl brings tea and sweets for the guests , SO the man and the girl see each other. Then the man's father and the girl's father talk about the amount of the dowry , AND the man's mother and the girl's mother discuss the time of the engagement party. Finally, the man puts the engagement ring on the girl's finger.

Mahmoud Shafaibajestan
Iran

Exercise 4E

Read the following paragraphs. Then, with a partner or a small group, do the exercises that follow each paragraph.

I

Marriage in Jordan

Marriage in my country has specific steps. The first of these is the age of the groom. He should be over twenty years old. Second, the groom must cover the requirements of the bride such as clothes, gold, and the wedding ceremony, so he must have a lot of money. <u>Then the groom thinks about a suitable wife for himself</u>. He looks for many things such as her culture, her beauty, her family, and her age, so the process takes a long time. After that, he finds a suitable wife, and he talks with his family. <u>It is very important to have the blessing of his family</u>. If he and his family agree, they go to the father of the bride, who has the power to give them the final decision. Finally, the two families agree on the marriage, and they plan the bridal day and the ceremony.

Basem Masaedeh
Jordan

1. Put parentheses ( ) around 5 time connectors in the paragraph.
2. Circle the subject (S) and circle the verb (V) in the <u>underlined</u> sentences.
3. Put a box around the | , and | and the | , so | that join two clauses.
4. What questions could you ask Basem about marriage in his country? How might he revise this paragraph? Could Basem write more than one paragraph about his topic?

II

Marriage Customs in Honduras

There are many steps to follow when two persons decide to get married in Honduras. First, there is an engagement that begins when the groom's parents ask the bride's parents for her hand. The groom always gives his bride a ring as a symbol of their union until they get married. For the engagement party, the man usually wears a suit. * The girl wears a beautiful pastel dress. This event usually takes place in the bride's house. * All the relatives of the young couple are invited. After that, there is a civil marriage in the District Center. * A few months after the civil marriage, the church ceremony takes place. The civil ceremony is performed by a lawyer. * The church ceremony is performed by a priest. In this ceremony, the young couple is united before God. * This is the most important part of the marriage. The clothes worn by the young couple are special clothes. The girl wears a long white dress with a veil covering her face. * The man wears a black or a white suit. Afterwards, the parents of the groom give a big party for all the relatives and friends of the young couple. Finally, the bride and the groom go on a trip for their honeymoon.

Olga Handal
Honduras

1. Join clauses with | , and | , | , but | or | , so | where you see the asterisks (*).
2. <u>Underline</u> 3 connectors in the paragraph.

3. Put parentheses ( ) around three adverbs of frequency.

4. (Circle) THERE IS and THERE ARE in the paragraph.
   Put the subjects of THERE IS and THERE ARE in brackets [ ].

III

Typical American Weddings

   In an American wedding, the bride and groom have control over the details of the wedding. However, a few basic elements are common to most weddings. A traditional wedding consists of six principle sections: the colors, a priest (or minister), the wedding vows, rings, the reception, and the honeymoon. Ordinarily, black and white are used as the basic colors in the wedding, the bride in white, and the groom in a black tuxedo, with bridesmaids wearing dresses that are a different and complementary color (which the bride has chosen). The bride and groom stand together before a priest (or minister), who reads their vows and conducts the ceremony. A vow is a promise of what each individual agrees to contribute to the marriage. After the completion of the vows, the bride and groom each place a ring on the other's left hand, usually on the third finger. Then customarily, they kiss. After the ceremony, a reception for both of the families and their guests is held; often excellent food is served, and the guests are able to dance to joyful music. Finally, the bride and groom leave for a trip by themselves, which is called the honeymoon, during which time they celebrate in privacy.

Joe Raicevich
United States

1. Put parentheses ( ) around 5 time connectors in the paragraph.

2. Underline 3 time connectors in the paragraph.

3. (Circle) the subject (S) and the verb (V) in the underlined sentences.

4. What U.S. wedding customs are similar to wedding customs in your culture? Which are different?

The first time I saw your face,
I felt it was the passing wind.
Now I know it is yearning for you.
When I trace your shadow,
when I see your face,
I belong to you.

translated by
Woo Seok Cheon
Korea

Writing Assignment

1. Write THREE paragraphs about marriage in your country. As you begin to plan your paragraphs, answer some of the following questions.

   Paragraph I: *How People in My Country Become Engaged*
   - Do the men and women in your country decide whom they should marry?
   - Do the parents in your country decide whom their sons and daughters should marry?
   - How is an engagement arranged?
     - First,…
     - Second,…
     - Then,…
     - Next, …
     - After that,…
     - Finally,…
   - Is there an engagement celebration?
   - Are gifts given? (By whom? What kind?)
   - How long is the engagement period?

   Paragraph II: *How the Bride Prepares for the Wedding*
   - Who helps the bride prepare for the wedding?
   - What plans are made?
     - First,…
     - Second,…
     - Then,…
     - Next,…
     - After that,…
     - Finally,…
   - Where will the wedding be held?
   - Who is invited to the wedding?

Paragraph III: *The Wedding Celebration*

- What do the bride and groom wear?
- How long does the celebration last?
- How is the wedding place decorated?
- What happens on the wedding day?
  - First,…
  - Second,…
  - Then,…
  - Next,…
  - After that,…
  - Finally,…
- What special foods are served?
- What special customs occur?

2. Exchange papers with a partner. As you read your partner's paragraphs, do the following:

   A. In the first paragraph (about engagements), <u>underline</u> the connectors.

   B. In the second paragraph (about planning the wedding), put a box around each ⌐, and⌐ , ⌐, but⌐ or ⌐, so⌐ that joins two clauses.

   C. In the third paragraph, put an asterisk (*) between 2 clauses that could be joined by *and, but,* or *so.*

   D. Ask your partner one question about each paragraph so that your partner can make her or his paragraph more complete and interesting.

3. Reread your paragraphs. How can you make your paragraphs more interesting? Use your own ideas and your classmate's questions to revise your paragraphs. Also, decide whether or not you want to join clauses in paragraph III where your partner put an asterisk (*). Next, rewrite your paragraphs.

4. Share your paragraphs with a small group of classmates. Read the paragraphs of two to four classmates. At the end of each of the student's paragraphs, write one sentence about what you liked about the paragraph, and one question that will help the author make his or her paragraph more interesting.

5. Reread your paragraphs. Use the questions of your classmates to make your paragraphs more detailed and more interesting. Revise and then rewrite your paragraphs.

> Appearing in her eyes there was a tear,
> and on my lips, a forgiving phrase.
> Pride spoke, and she dried her tear,
> and the phrase on my lips expired.
> I follow one road, she follows another,
> but when thinking of our mutual love
> I say even now, "Why didn't I speak that day?"
> And she would say, "Why didn't I cry?"
>
> translated by
> *Gustavo Garcia*
> Ecuador

Exercise 4F

With a partner or a small group of classmates, read the following paragraphs. Then do the exercises that follow each paragraph.

I

A Holiday Celebration in My Country

In Sweden we have a very special custom called *Lucia*. We always celebrate it on December 13th, the darkest and coldest time of year in Sweden. <u>The sun rarely shines.</u> * It is as cold as −30°C. Then, in the early morning of December 13th, she comes: Lucia, the symbol of hope that the light will return after the long winter darkness. <u>She wears a crown of candles in her hair.</u> * The crown spreads light and warmth everywhere she goes. She also wears a long, snow-white dress with a bright red ribbon around her waist. She sings traditional songs. * She usually serves coffee and saffron-buns and gingerbread biscuits to "thaw the frozen hearts of the Swedes."

Cecilia Larsson
Sweden

1. Join clauses with `, and` where you see the asterisks (*).
2. (Circle) the subject (S) and the verb (V) in each of the <u>underlined</u> sentences.
3. Put parentheses ( ) around three adverbs of frequency.
4. What questions might you ask Cecilia about the celebration of *Lucia*? How could she make her paragraph more interesting?

II

A Holiday Celebration in the United States

It's a very special time when my family gets together for Christmas in late December. In my home, there is always a big, fluffy pine tree in the living room. It is decorated beautifully with different colored lights and colored glass balls. My family usually decorates our tree while we sing our favorite Christmas songs. We put each ornament neatly in place. Then it is time to await the visit of Saint Nick (whom some call Santa Claus). On Christmas morning, there are many presents strewn underneath the tree. Everyone gets up early. * When all of the presents have been opened, we get ready for company. We all take showers, clean the house, and set the table. My mother has been up since early in the morning, cooking turkey. Our guests often begin arriving about noon. Many of our relatives have traveled a long way to see us. * We share a wonderful meal of turkey, stuffing, mashed potatoes and gravy, green salad, various other salads, and cranberry sauce. We talk about our lives, sharing joys and sorrow well into the evening, having a good time with people we love.

Luke Malyurek
United States

1. Join clauses with | , and | where you see the asterisks (*).
2. Circle the subject (S) and the verb (V) in each of the underlined sentences.
3. Put parentheses ( ) around three adverbs of frequency.
4. What questions can you ask Luke about his paragraph? How could he make his paragraph more interesting?

Bad weeds never die.

Aaron Berman
United States

Other Writing Topics

Plan and write one or more paragraphs about your country. Remember to use specific detail that will interest your audience. You might use some of the topics below for your paragraph.

- My Favorite Dinner in My Country

- Party Food in My Country

- My Favorite Restaurant

- A Game Children Play in My Country

- How Parents Spend Their Leisure Time in My Country

- How Teenagers Spend Their Leisure Time in My Country

- How People Spend Their Vacations in My Country

- Special Slang Used by Secondary School Students in My Country

- Special Clothes Worn by Secondary School Students in My Country

- Foreign Languages Studied in My Country

- Dating Customs in My Country

- Important School Subjects for Boys and Girls in My Country

- Burial Traditions in My Country

- _____

Writing Projects

Individual Project: Make a booklet about your country's culture. Use the paragraph(s) that you wrote for the assignment above, and use some of the paragraphs you wrote and revised in this chapter. Write some other paragraphs about other cultural activities in your country. You might write about some of the paragraph topics that are listed.

- A Hero From My Country

- A Famous Book From My Country

- A Famous Piece of Art in My Country

- A Famous Poet in My Country

- A Popular Movie Actor or Actress from My Country

- A Popular Contemporary Musician from My Country

- _____

Remember that your audience probably doesn't know very much about your country and culture. Use specific detail that will be <u>clear</u> and <u>interesting</u> for your audience. That may mean that you must write more than one paragraph about a topic.

You might also translate some sayings or short poems from your country/culture into English (just as other students have translated sayings and short poems in this textbook), and include them in your booklet. Or, with another classmate from your language and cultural background, you might translate a folk tale from your country.

Decorate your booklet with drawings, maps, and photographs about your country. Ask the Office of International Services to display your booklet during International Week, and/or present the booklet to the public library.

Group Project: With your classmates, make a recipe booklet of international foods. Collect recipes and directions for cooking the foods from classmates and friends. Be sure to do the following:

- Put a list of cooking abbreviations at the beginning of the booklet.
- Make a table of contents for the booklets: list the name of each recipe and the page on which it appears.
- Use illustrations to demonstrate some of the tasks.

Remember that your audience needs <u>specific directions</u> for each recipe. Ask friends NOT in your class (or classmates) to read the recipes and ask questions about the directions and the materials for each recipe. Then revise your recipes to make them clearer.

Decorate the recipe book with drawings or photographs. Then have a party for the class, and cook the foods. Present a copy of the recipe booklet to the local or the university newspaper. Give permission to print the recipes in the newspaper.

5

Travel Experiences

Preparing for My Trip

On August 6, the *New Nigerian Newspaper* listed me as a participant in an educational training program, so I quickly prepared to travel. At that time, my country banned new passports, but I went to the Ministry of Education in Lagos, Nigeria. The minister issued me a passport and other documents. Then I went to the American Embassy in Lagos, and the people there were very helpful. After that, I returned to my village to inform my parents and other relatives about my trip, and they all prayed for me. On August 25, I finally boarded the plane for my new life.

Sanni B. Mounde
Nigeria

PAST TENSE (-ed) SPELLING FOR REGULAR VERBS*

Consonant + e (-d)

prepar*e* ⟶ prepare*d*
arri*ve* ⟶ arriv*ed*

Vowel + 1 consonant
(double the final consonant + -ed)

st*op* ⟶ stop*ped*
trav*el* ⟶ travel*led*

2 Consonants (-ed)

fini*sh* ⟶ finish*ed*
wa*lk* ⟶ walk*ed*

2 Vowels + 1 consonant (-ed)

n*eed* ⟶ need*ed*
w*ait* ⟶ wait*ed*

Consonant + y (y -ied)
(drop y + -ied)

stu*dy* ⟶ stud*ied*
wor*ry* ⟶ worr*ied*

Vowel + y (-ed)

enj*oy* ⟶ enjoy*ed*
pl*ay* ⟶ play*ed*

*See Appendix D for spelling rules.

How I Prepared for a Trip

Last year, I <u>prepared</u> carefully for my vacation trip. First, I <u>wanted</u> to know more about the city, so I <u>asked</u> my friends about it. Then I made my travel reservations, and I <u>counted</u> my money. Next, I <u>packed</u> my camera and my clothes. Finally, I <u>looked</u> at some pictures, and I <u>studied</u> a map of the city.

Harijano Tedjo
Indonesia

The moon of foreign countries is bigger than the moon in our own country.

translated by
Hsiang-Rwei Tseng
Taiwan (R.O.C.)

Exercise 5A

Read the following paragraphs. Write the correct form of the past tense verbs in the blanks. Then do the exercises that follow each paragraph.

I

Preparing for a Trip

Before I came to the United States, I _____ very busy preparing for
be
all the things that I _____ . It took about a month for me to get ready. First,
need
I went to Kuala Lumpur (that is the capital city of Malaysia) to get a visa. <u>My</u>

<u>sponsor gave me important documents.</u> After that, I _____ to my town, and I
return
_____ the doctor for a medical check-up. <u>The doctor gave me a health</u>
visit
<u>certificate.</u> My mother was also busy making dresses for me. She _____ a lot
sew
of dresses. <u>I also bought some books in my language.</u> <u>For example, I bought a</u>

<u>dictionary and some religious books.</u> Besides that I _____ some spices and
pack
preserved food. <u>Finally, I _____ my relatives to say goodbye.</u>
visit

Noorazian Ariffin
Malaysia

1. Identify the subjects (S) and the verbs (V) in the <u>underlined</u> sentences.
2. (Circle) 5 connectors in the paragraph.
3. What do you remember about the paragraph?
4. Is the writer male or female? How do you know?

II

Preparing for My Trip to the Philippines

Before I left Sri Lanka to travel to the Philippines, I _____ to make
have
certain preparations. <u>First, I _____ my passport, visa, medical documents, air</u>
obtain
<u>ticket, and traveller's checks.</u> Then I _____ the materials I would need, such
gather
as clothes, writing materials, and books. After that, I made a list, and
I _____ all the needed things in bags. <u>I also _____ mentally for my trip.</u>
pack   **prepare**
I told myself, "When you are there, maybe no one will be friendly to you. If you are

rejected, can you stand it?" <u>My mental answer _____ that I could</u>. So I found
be

a strong and favorable mental attitude that helped me to remain happy in a new

country that is very different from my country.

M. Gunawardena
Sri Lanka

1. Identify the subjects (S) and the verbs (V) in the <u>underlined</u> sentences.
2. (Circle) 3 time connectors in the paragraph.
3. What is the main idea in the paragraph? How do you know?
4. What was the most important preparation made by the author? How do you know?

III

_____

    When I _____ my admission from a university in the United States,
        receive

I _____ very happy. I tried to become as informed as possible about the
 be

American lifestyle. First, I _____ to foreign people who had visited the
                talk

U.S.A., and I _____ to U.S. radio stations. Of course, I also wrote a few
       listen

letters to some Moroccan students in the U.S. I _____ that the U.S. had
                     learn

chilly weather, so I bought some heavy coats, and my mother _____ some
                                   pack

medicines and hot spices to prevent illness. Then I _____ to bring some
                      decide

typical and traditional things with me like Moroccan songs, clothes, and my

family pictures. I also _____ English a little. After that, I _____ all
      study   **obtain**

my administrative papers. Finally, I went to three different cities to say goodbye

to some of my closest friends.

M'Hamed Jebbanema
Morocco

1. Put boxes around the 「 , and 」 and the 「 , so 」 that join two clauses. (Circle) the subjects in each of the clauses.

2. <u>Underline</u> 5 time connectors.

3. Write a title for the paragraph.

4. Why did the author take some traditional things with him to the U.S.?

> A cheap purchase is money lost.
>
> translated by
> *Mari Kanada*
> Japan

Exercise 5B

With a partner, read the following paragraphs. Then do the exercises that follow each paragraph.

I

Preparing for a Trip

When I came to the UPLB in the Philippines, I first _____ a visa from
receive
the Philippine Embassy in Thailand. Then I _____ the papers for my field of
complete
study, and I _____ my friend who was studying at UPLB. After that, I
contact
_____ my personal belongings. I did not bring a suit and a necktie because in
prepare
the Philippines, people usually use informal dress like the American style. The Thai

foods that I brought were dry chili, dry sweet pork, Thai chili sauce, and some dry

desserts. I also _____ some Thai souvenirs, cigarette cases and ladies'
pack
necklaces, for my advisory committee and my Filipino friends. Finally, I met

respected relatives to say goodbye, and I _____ some good wishes from them.
receive
The day I left, I paid respect to my Lord Buddha, and my parents took photographs

of my family and the people who came to the airport.

Samakkee Boonyawat
Thailand

1. Write the correct past tense verbs in the blanks.

2. (Circle) the articles in the paragraph.

3. Put boxes around the [, and] that joins two clauses. <u>Underline</u> the subject in each of the clauses in those sentences.

4. Why did the author pack some souvenirs?

II

Preparing for My Future

I was awarded a fellowship, so I _____ to study in the United States
                                  decide
of America. However, I _____ about three things. First, my friends told me
                 worry
about the cold winter, so I _____ a few winter clothes. Secondly, I
                      purchase
_____ for my family to stay in India for the year I would be gone. Third, I am
arrange
a vegetarian, and I was afraid that I would not be able to eat as I travelled, so I

_____ some food for my journey.
   pack

Ashok Kumar Hebbar
India

1. Write the correct past tense verbs in the blanks.

2. Put parentheses ( ) around 5 prepositional phrases in the paragraph.
   (Circle) the noun (or the pronoun) that follows each preposition.

3. Put boxes around [, and] and [, so] in the paragraph. <u>Underline</u> the subject for each of the clauses in those sentences.

4. What questions could you ask the author about the preparations he made for his trip? Could the author write more than one paragraph about his topic? What other paragraphs could he write?

III

Leaving My Village

One windy and sunny summer morning, my father _____ me and
my grandmother into his private room. He told us that, like every eighteen-year-
old in my village, I must go to France. The following day, my father
_____ all the village elders, and he told them about my departure. The

morning of my departure, my father slaughtered a white cock, whose blood would protect me during my trip. Then he broke three cola nuts. Next to him stood my grandmother, who was very concerned about the trip. She spit on my head and gave me a bracelet that had belonged to her father before he died. This bracelet _____ a token for me to remember her by. At ten o'clock the wagon was ready, and I sat beside the driver. Immediately, my father _____ pouring holy water behind the horses, and he said, "I pray you, God, bless him." He continued until we drove off. I _____ my left hand because, according to our custom, a man does not wave his right hand while he is leaving to go abroad. Thus, I left my native village with great ceremony.

VERBS: start   be   summon   call   wave

Issaka Sarr
Mali

1. Write the correct regular past tense verb in the blanks. Use each verb on the list only once.
2. Put parentheses ( ) around 5 prepositional phrases in the paragraph.
3. What do you remember about the paragraph?
4. What questions could you ask Issaka about this paragraph? Could Issaka write more than one paragraph about this topic?

Writing Assignment

Write a paragraph describing your preparations for a long trip. Use the chart below to plan your paragraph. Use | , and |, | , but | or | , so | to join two clauses in several of the sentences.

How I Prepared For A Long Trip

First, I _____

Second, I _____

Then I _____

After that, I _____

Next, I _____

Then I _____

Finally, I _____

1. Exchange paragraphs with a classmate. Read your classmate's paragraph.

2. Then:

   A. Underline the past tense verbs.

   B. Put each prepositional phrase in parentheses ( ).

   C. Put boxes around each | , and | , | , but | or | , so | joining two clauses.

   D. Circle the connectors in the paragraph.

3. Ask your classmate two questions about his or her preparation that will make the paragraph more interesting.

4. Use your partner's questions to revise your paragraph.

5. Finally, share your rewritten paragraph with a small group of classmates.

My life, which was like two or three days, is gone,
as fast as the water in the brook
and the wind in the valley.
I never worry about two days:
the day which has gone,
and the day which is not here yet.

translated by
Keyvan Karbassiyon
Iran

IRREGULAR VERBS—PAST TENSE (EXAMPLES)*

Present	Past	Present	Past
begin	began	know	knew
break	broke	leave	left
bring	brought	make	made
buy	bought	say	said
come	came	see	saw
feel	felt	sit	sat
find	found	speak	spoke
fly	flew	stand	stood
get	got	spend	spent
give	gave	take	took
go	went	teach	taught
hang	hung	tell	told

*See Appendix A for a list of regular and irregular verbs.

Preparing for a Long Trip

Like almost all men in our traditional African society, I prepared for the major trip which led me out of my country by informing the people in my village. First, as our customs require, I visited the chief of the village, and I informed him about my decision to leave for another country. He <u>GAVE</u> me permission to go, and he advised me not to forget the relatives I was about to leave. What I did next was to consult the Imam of the mosque. Since I acted according to tradition, I <u>BROUGHT</u> him some cola nuts, and he blessed me by reading some verses from the Koran. After that, I <u>WENT</u> from family to family, and I <u>TOLD</u> them that I was planning to travel. Those who had some relatives in the country I was going to <u>GAVE</u> me letters and asked me to transmit their greetings to their relatives. Thus, I fulfilled the conditions which all men in our society must fulfill before traveling, and I <u>LEFT</u> for my first long trip.

Cheick F. M. Kante
Mali

Exercise 5C

With a partner, read the following paragraphs. Write the present tense verb ABOVE each of the <u>underlined</u> past tense irregular verbs. Then do the exercises that follow.

I

An Adventure!

When I was flying from Magadishu Airport to the U.S., I <u>felt</u> very nervous, and I was so sad about leaving my family. It <u>was</u> not the first time for me to fly in an airplane, but it was the longest trip that I had taken. However, it was an adventure for me to fly for over twenty hours. For example, I was amazed when I experienced jet lag between my country and the U.S.A., and I also experienced it between New York and Missouri. Since it was a very long trip, I felt light-headed. I also <u>felt</u> my ears popping, and, of course, I experienced motion sickness. In fact, when I arrived in the U.S.A., I <u>was</u> so tired that I slept almost three days!

Abdirizak Osman
Somalia

1. (Circle) the subjects for the <u>underlined</u> irregular past tense verbs.
2. Put boxes around the , and and , but that join two clauses.
3. Put parentheses ( ) around 5 articles.
4. What does Abdirizak mean by "jet lag"?

II

When I Flew to the U.S.A.

On the afternoon of September 8, I <u>took</u> an airplane and left my country, Taiwan.   First I <u>flew</u> to Japan, and I stayed there about one hour. * Then I transferred to another airplane to go to San Francisco.   I was sitting between two Chinese men. * I did not have any conversation with these neighbors.   I was overwhelmed with grief and apprehension about leaving my mother and my boyfriend.   As the airplane flew through the air, I <u>held</u> back my tears and tried to read. * I <u>felt</u> uncomfortable and nauseous.   I <u>spent</u> about fourteen hours in the airplane.   * I could not sleep because it was too terrible.   Although I was going to a new place, I felt anxious and queasy.   All in all, I think my flight to the United States <u>was</u> a bad experience.

Hui-Ching Chiang
Taiwan (R.O.C.)

1. (Circle) the subject for the <u>underlined</u> irregular past tense verbs.
2. Write , and or , but to join two clauses where you see the asterisks (*).
3. Put parentheses ( ) around 2 negative verbs in the paragraph.
4. Do not look again at the paragraph. Tell your partner what you remember about the ideas in the paragraph. What **memorable detail** did you remember?

III

Preparation for a Trip

When I was preparing for my trip to Europe, to see my brother, who was in the Army, I had to do many different things. I was in school at the time. * First I had to get ahead in all of my school work so that I didn't have to worry about it during my trip. Then I had to go and get a passport, so that I could travel to another country. After that I had to get my plane ticket. * It was really expensive. Finally, a couple of days before I left, I had to start packing for the trip. Because I was going to be gone for two weeks, I had to think about what I would wear and make sure I had enough of everything. After I finished all of that, I got on the plane and was on my way.

Lance Lewis
United States

1. (Circle) 3 connectors in the paragraph.
2. Write |, and| or |, so| to join two clauses where you see the asterisks (*).
3. Put parentheses ( ) around 5 prepositional phrases.
4. What questions could you ask Lance about his paragraph? How could he make his paragraph more interesting?

> If you don't go to the tiger's cave,
> how can you catch the cub?
>
> translated by
> *Prayat Laoprapossone*
> Thailand

Interview

Ask a person (perhaps a person NOT in your class) to describe a trip that he or she took. Use the questions that follow to help plan the interview.

- Where did you go?

- How did you get there?

- Why did you go there?

- What did you do first?

- What did you do next?

- Then what did you do?

- After that, what did you do?

- Did you enjoy the trip?

Ask your friend any other necessary questions to complete an interesting paragraph.

1. Then write the paragraph about your friend's trip.
   - use regular and irregular past tense verbs
   - use time connectors
   - in some sentences, join two clauses with | , and | , | , but | or | , so | .
2. Exchange paragraphs with a classmate. Read that paragraph.
3. Then:
   - underline the regular and irregular past tense verbs.
   - circle the subject pronouns.
   - put boxes around the | , and | , | , but | or | , so | that join two clauses.
4. Tell your partner what **memorable detail** you liked most in the paragraph.

> It is easy to move mountains and seas,
> but it is difficult to change one's character.
>
> translated by
> *John Shyh-Yuan Wang*
> China (P R.C.)

VERBS OF FEELING + ADJECTIVES

	Present			**Past**	
	Verb	**Adjective**		**Verb**	**Adjective**
I	feel	happy.	I	felt	(very) lonely.
He She	>seem*s* }	frightened.	He She	>seem*ed* }	unhappy.
You	look	(very) angry.	You	look*ed*	sick.
We	become	nervous.	We	became	sad.
They	are	kind.	They	were	tired.

Leaving

Before I left my country to come to the U.S.A., I <u>WAS</u> very <u>UNCOMFORTABLE</u> because I had to leave my family. When I was at the airport, I <u>WAS NERVOUS</u> because this was the first time I was going to leave my family. After I said goodbye to my family, I went to the airplane, but I <u>FELT UNHAPPY</u>. At the moment that the airplane was starting to move, I <u>FELT TERRIBLE</u>. When the airplane was in the air, I saw my country through the window. It <u>LOOKED</u> so <u>SMALL</u> that it looked like a map. The flight attendant gave me my food and a cup of tea. After that, I took a nap. When I woke up, I found myself in Washington. I <u>WAS AMAZED</u> because the time went by so fast. At the same time, I <u>FELT COLD</u>, <u>SCARED</u>, and <u>HOMESICK</u> already.

Ameen Alawi
United Arab Emirates

Exercise 5D

With a small group of classmates, read the following paragraphs. Then do the exercises that follow each paragraph.

I

Leaving My Family

I do not want to think about the day I left my country. I felt sad about leaving my family and my friends. * It was a very bad day. I wanted to stay with them. * The airplane was waiting for me. My body felt tight because I did not want to leave. I saw my family. * I began to think, "Is this the way I should follow or not? What will happen to me when I leave my family?" Before this trip, I had travelled for just a few weeks. * This time I was not returning for five years or more. My mother was very sad. * I held her because I did not want her to cry. I held my father, my brothers, and my sisters. Then I said goodbye.

Mohamed Gaddah
Morocco

1. <u>Underline</u> 3 verbs of feeling + 3 adjectives of feeling in the paragraph.

2. Put parentheses ( ) around 3 prepositional phrases in the paragraph.

3. Write ⏍, and⏎ , ⏍, but⏎ or ⏍, so⏎ to join two clauses where you see the asterisks (*).

4. Discuss Mohamed's feelings with your group. Which **memorable detail** helps you "feel" his sadness?

II

The Miami Airport

When I arrived at the airport in Miami, it was the night before Christmas. First, I looked for a telephone to call my friend. * I got lost. I became frightened. When I tried to ask for help, the people did not understand me, so I felt frustrated. Finally, I found a telephone. * I called my friend. However, she told me that she could not pick me up because she was sick. I felt so sad and lonely. Then I spent Christmas eve and Christmas morning at the Miami airport. I was very angry. * I wanted to go back to my country.

Silvia C. Higuera
Colombia

1. <u>Underline</u> 4 verbs + their 4 adjectives of feeling in the paragraph.

2. (Circle) 4 regular past tense verbs.

3. Join two clauses with ⏍, and⏎ , ⏍, but⏎ or ⏍, so⏎ where you see the asterisks (*).

4. Have you ever had an experience like Silvia's? Discuss that experience with your group.

III

Angry and Happy

After the plane landed in Tucson, Arizona, I _____ to telephone my
want
parents' friends, but I did not know the spelling of their last name. I _____ the
call

operator, and I _____ my problem. She said, "I cannot give you a telephone
        explain

number if you do not know the spelling of the last name." Then I _____ "I
        say

think that the first letter is Y." She said, "I do not know. I do not know." Then she

_____ up. That _____ me so angry. After that, I _____ very
  hang   **make**   **feel**

anxious, but I _____ to try again. This time, the new operator _____
       decide   **be**

very kind, and she _____ Spanish! I _____ very happy to hear her
       speak   **feel**

voice, and she _____ me locate my parents' friends.
       help

Sandra Fuñes
El Salvador

1. Write the correct regular and irregular past tense verbs in the blanks.
2. Circle 5 negative verbs in the paragraph.
3. Put parentheses ( ) around 4 connectors.
4. Why is the title of this paragraph "Angry and Happy"?

Patience is bitter, but it has a sweet fruit.

translated by
Keyvan Karbassiyon
Iran

Interview

    Ask a person NOT in your class to describe his or her feelings when he or she took a long airplane trip. Write a paragraph about the information you receive.

1. As you plan your paragraph, ask some of these questions:
   - How did you feel at first?
   - How did you feel at the airport?
   - How did you feel when the plane took off?
   - How did you feel during the flight?
   - How did you feel after that?
   - How did you feel when you arrived at your destination?

2. Write a paragraph about that person's feelings.
   A. Use correct object and subject pronouns.
   B. Use regular and irregular past tense verbs.
   C. Use connectors.
   D. In some sentences, join two clauses with `, and`, `, but` or `, so`.

3. Exchange paragraphs with a classmate. Read the paragraph.
   A. Underline the regular and irregular past tense verbs.
   B. Put a box around the `, and`, `, but` or `, so` that joins two clauses.
   C. Circle the verbs of feeling + the adjectives.
   D. Are there any questions you could ask your classmate about the paragraph?

> One time of seeing is better
> than one hundred times of asking.
>
> translated by
> *Kyu-Yong Lee*
> Korea

Exercise 5E

With a small group of classmates, read the following paragraphs. Then do the exercises that follow each paragraph.

I

Our Arrival in the United States

My family _____ from Vietnam. We _____ to the United
      escape   **fly**
States safely from the enemies below us. Many of the airplanes trying to

escape _____ shot down, but our airplane did not get caught.
    be
God _____ us through safely. After we arrived, we _____ to an
   help   **go**
immigrant camp in Arkansas. We did not plan to stay there. It _____ a camp
                            be
for immigrants to live until they _____ their friends, family, or sponsor. Even
              contact
though my own people _____ all around me, I did not feel comfortable.
              be
However, my family was lucky to get the best room in the apartment. It was the only

room that had a door and privacy. Other rooms _____ wooden walls that did
              have
not reach to the ceiling, but just _____ them into little compartments. That
           divide
first week _____ an experience for me. I _____ new things to expect in
    be   **learn**
the United States, and I also _____ to speak the American language. One
             begin
thing that I was sad about was that my father was not there to share the experience.

Thao Nguyen
Vietnam

1. Write the correct regular and irregular past tense verbs in the blanks.
2. Put boxes around each ⬚ , and or ⬚ , but that joins two clauses. (Circle) the subject for each clause.
3. Put parentheses ( ) around 2 verbs + adjectives of feeling in the paragraph.
4. How was Thao's trip different from trips described in the other paragraphs in this chapter? Discuss your answer with your small group of classmates.

II

_____

I was in an airplane flying from Mexico to the United States to start a new experience in my life. A lot of thoughts _____ to my mind while I watched the volcanoes around my city become smaller and smaller. At last, all I could see was the white snow on the tops of the mountains. "Now you have to look forward," I said to myself. My home had disappeared, and a new country was waiting for me just a few hours ahead. The faces of my father, mother, and sisters were clear in my mind, telling me "Good luck!" I was excited because I always _____ to live overseas in order to see how people behave and to understand another culture. Though I was not sure about my English, I _____ that I was able to express myself. I could talk with American students and make good friends in the U.S. But I knew that I would face many challenges, and that I had to take advantage of this new part of my life. So I _____ ready to learn as much as possible during the next few months.

VERBS: know   come   want   be

Fernando Menesez
Mexico

1. Write the correct regular and irregular past tense verbs in the blanks.

2. Put boxes around each ⌈ , and ⌉ or ⌈ , but ⌉ that joins two clauses. (Circle) the subject for each clause.

3. With your group, write a title for this paragraph.

4. What questions could you and your group ask Fernando to help him make his paragraph more interesting?

NEGATIVE PAST TENSE

Regular Verbs			
I	wanted	I	*did not* want*
He		He	
She	visited	She	*did not* visit*
It		It	
You	studied	You	*did not* study*
We	stayed	We	*did not* stay*
They	helped	They	*did not* help*

*The negative takes the root form of the verb.

Lost!

I arrived at J. F. Kennedy Airport with a group of Finnish students, and we DID NOT KNOW where to go. We DID NOT FIND the terminal for our connecting flight. We asked some people, but they DID NOT UNDERSTAND us. The airport was as big as a city, but we finally found our flight. When we arrived in Washington, D.C., we DID NOT KNOW how to reach the hotel. The street system was so different, and there were so many people. Some of the people were nice to us, so we found our hotel. We DID NOT HAVE to sleep on the street!

Katrina Lahtinen
Finland

Exercise 5F

With a partner, read the following paragraphs. Then do the exercises that follow each paragraph.

I

Competence and Incompetence

Life in the United States encourages people to become competent. I did not realize how important being useful and competent was for me until I went to Taiwan. When our plane landed, I decided to smile through all the experiences that we would have. However, because I did not know the Chinese language, I immediately _____ to have problems. First, our friend did not meet us at the airport. I tried to telephone him, but I could not get the telephone to work. A gentleman _____ to me in Mandarin Chinese. I did not understand him, so he took the number I had written, and he telephoned my friend. However, he obviously _____ that I was not very intelligent. Then, as we were waiting for our friend, I _____ useless. I was not competent in this new world, and so I had no worth. Later that evening, as we were walking along the streets to our new apartment, I started to cry. I was standing in the middle of the street, stating loudly (in English) that I wanted to go home!

VERBS: speak   feel   begin   think

Lois Thomas
United States

1. Write the correct irregular past tense verbs in the blanks. Use each verb on the list only once.

2. Put parentheses ( ) around the negative verbs in the paragraph.

3. Is this a good title for the paragraph? Why or why not? Discuss your answer with your partner.

4. What do you remember about this paragraph? Why? Discuss your answer with your partner.

II

_____

After I _____ in Washington, D.C., I _____ to the hotel that had
arrive   **go**
been reserved for me by my sponsor. I _____ to walk from my hotel to a
                                        have
restaurant to eat. * I did not _____ the task. The complexity of the city roads,
                        like
the large number of vehicles, and the frightening traffic lights made crossing the

road a terrible thing for me.   I was very frightened by the cars because

I _____ that they would crash into me. Therefore, I was very worried about
  assume
my life during my first weeks in the United States. I did not _____ friends to
                                                        have
contact in case I had an accident in Washington. * I was very careful whenever I

had to cross streets. Unfortunately, that _____ that I always had to wait a very
                                    mean
long time before crossing.   Because of my experiences in Washington,

I _____ that in the U.S.A., one should own a car, and one should never walk
  decide
anywhere!

Hailu Kenno
Ethiopia

1. Write the correct regular and irregular past tense verbs in the blanks.
   Remember, the root form of the verb is used with the negative.
2. Use ⌐ , but ⌐ or ⌐ , so ⌐ to join two clauses where you see the asterisks (*).
   (Circle) the   subject for each clause.

3. With your partner, write a title for this paragraph.
4. What frightened Hailu? Discuss your answer with your partner.

Writing Assignment

Write a paragraph about how you felt when you began a long trip.

1. As you plan your paragraph, use some of the statements in the chart that
   follows.

How I Felt When I Began a Long Trip

I felt_____   because_____

For example, _____

Then I felt _____   because_____

For example, _____

After that, I felt _____   because_____

For example, _____

I also felt _____   because_____

For example, _____

2. As you write your paragraph,

   A. use connectors

   B. use some regular and irregular past tense verbs

   C. try to use some adjectives of feeling in your paragraph

3. When you have finished writing your paragraph, exchange paragraphs with a classmate. Read that paragraph, and do the following:

   A. underline the regular and irregular past tense verbs

   B. circle the connectors

   C. put boxes around the $\boxed{\text{, and}}$, $\boxed{\text{, but}}$ or $\boxed{\text{, so}}$ that joins two clauses

4. Are there any questions you could ask your classmate about the paragraph?

5. Now, reread your paragraph. What could you add to your paragraph to make it more interesting?

Collaborative Writing Assignment

With a partner, study the graph on page 134. Then write <u>one</u> paragraph that describes the chart. As you and your partner plan your paragraph, use some of the sentence structures that are listed.

- According to the Institute of International Education,...

- For example, more than (X) percent of international graduate student engineers in U.S. universities...

- Moreover, (X) percent..., and (X) percent...

- Some international graduate student engineers (X percent)...

- We think that there are so many international graduate student engineers at U.S. universities because...

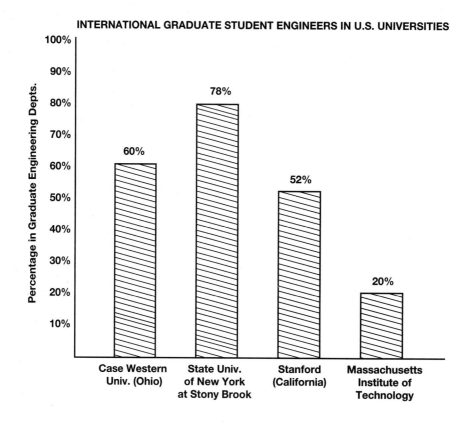

INTERNATIONAL GRADUATE STUDENT ENGINEERS IN U.S. UNIVERSITIES

Case Western Univ. (Ohio): 60%
State Univ. of New York at Stony Brook: 78%
Stanford (California): 52%
Massachusetts Institute of Technology: 20%

Friends are too many when you count them, but they are too few when you need them.

translated by
Adel Salameh
Iran

Exercise 5G

With a partner or a small group of students, read the following paragraphs. Then do the exercises that follow each paragraph.

I

Welcome to the United States!

My uncle and his family were waiting for my wife and me when our plane _____ in San Francisco. We _____ very tired and dirty from our long trip. * My uncle made us feel very happy. He greeted us warmly. * My uncle _____ us. He took us to his car. * He _____ us to his home. During the drive, he showed us the Golden Gate Bridge and other famous sights. When we _____ at his home, we relieved our fatigue by taking long baths and sleeping. My wife _____ that she did not want to leave my uncle's home!

VERBS: arrive   drive   feel   help   land   say

Jun-Chul Shin
Korea

1. Write the correct regular and irregular past tense verbs in the blanks. Use each verb only once.
2. Write | , and | or | , but | to join two clauses where you see the asterisks (*).
3. (Circle) 5 possessive adjectives in the paragraph.
4. Why was Shin's arrival in the United States a pleasant experience? Have you had a similar experience? Discuss your answers with your partner or your small group of classmates.

II

My Anxious Feelings

When the plane landed in Los Angeles, I was very anxious. I had to face a new situation. * I did not know how to predict it. First, I had to stay with my uncle. * I had not met him before. I did not know whether he was a kind or a fierce man. * I did not know what his wife and children thought about me. A lot of questions came to my mind. In addition, my uncle and his family were Chinese, but I spoke Thai. I spoke Chinese just a little, but I could not communicate with his family because the Chinese I spoke was different from the Chinese my uncle's family spoke. Finally, this was the first time I had been away from my parents, and I had to decide everything by myself. That thought made me feel afraid. Therefore, as my plane landed, I was very anxious.

Suttinun Chivakunakorn
Thailand

1. Write , and , , but or , so to join two clauses where you see the asterisks (*).

2. <u>Underline</u> 4 negative verbs.

3. Why was Suttinun anxious about her arrival?

4. What advice could you and your partner or group give Suttinun to help her?

III

_____

I was so tired when I arrived in Portland after fourteen hours on airplanes, but that was just the beginning of my troubles. First, I hoped that my friend would meet me at the airport because I _____ anything
                                                     (negative) know
about the United States. I _____ how to leave the airport. I
             (negative) understand
_____ what to do next. Where was my luggage? I followed the
   (negative) know
crowd, and I finally found my bags. Then I discovered that it was raining outside, and it was cold. I _____ warm clothes, and
                                    (negative) have
_____ where my friend lived. Finally, a kind gentleman
  (negative) remember
showed me how to use the telephone book and the pay telephone, and at about midnight I was able to talk with my friend.

Chia-Chieh Chen
Taiwan (R.O.C.)

1. Write the correct negative past tense verbs in the blanks.

2. Put parentheses ( ) around 4 connectors in the paragraph.

3. With your partner or your group, write a title for this paragraph.

4. What feelings do you think Chia-Chieh had when he arrived? Have you had a similar experience? Discuss your answers with your partner or your group.

Writing Assignment

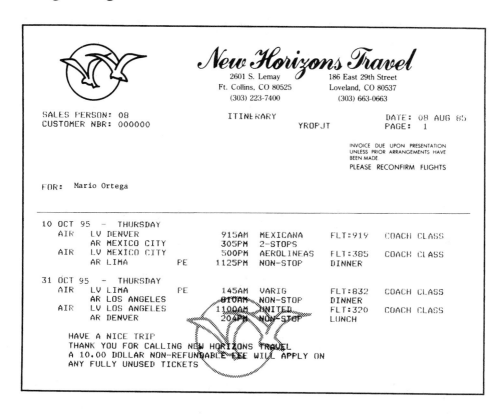

With a partner, study the flight schedule above. It shows Mario's trip to his home in Peru. Write <u>one</u> paragraph about his trip.

1. As you and your partner plan your paragraph, answer some of the following questions:
   - Where did Mario begin his trip?
   - What airline did Mario fly first?
   - When did he leave?
   - Where did he go first?
   - How long did his first flight take?
   - What airline did Mario fly second?
   - How long did he wait at his first stop?
   - When did his next flight leave?
   - When did he arrive in Lima, Peru?

- How long did his trip take?
- What feelings do you think that Mario had when he arrived?

2. As you and your partner write your paragraph,

   A. use past tense verbs

   B. use appropriate connectors

3. Exchange paragraphs with another set of partners. Read the paragraph with your partner, and

   A. underline the past tense verbs

   B. (circle) the connectors

   C. put parentheses ( ) around adjectives of feeling in the paragraph.

> The grass is always greener on the other side of the fence.
>
> *Harriet Fidler*
> United States

Interview

Ask a person NOT in your class to describe a long trip he or she took. Then write a paragraph describing that person's trip. Try to make it as interesting as you can.

1. As you begin to plan your paragraph, ask some of these questions:
   - Where did you go?
   - How long did you travel?
   - Did you have to change planes? Where?
   - Did you have any problems with the plane? What were they?
   - What other difficulties did you have?
   - How did you feel?
   - What problems did you solve? How?
   - What feelings did you have when you arrived? Why?

2. As you write your paragraph,
   A. use the correct subject and object pronouns
   B. use connectors
   C. use adjectives of feeling

3. Exchange paragraphs with a classmate. Read your partner's paragraph, and

   A. <u>underline</u> the regular and irregular past tense verbs

   B. put parentheses ( ) around the connectors in the paragraph

   C. (circle) the adjectives of feeling in the paragraph

   D. put brackets [ ] around any language errors you find

   E. ask your partner some questions that will make the paragraph more interesting

4. Now, reread your paragraph. What changes can you make in order to make your paragraph more interesting? Use your partner's suggestions.

5. Rewrite your paragraph.

A camel led by a camel, and a man led by a woman, cannot step aside from you.

> translated by
> *Mohamud Fahie*
> Somalia

Other Writing Topics

- My Last Day in My Country

- My Happiest Childhood Memory

- What I Did Yesterday

- A Fear I Had When I Was a Child

- An Accident I Remember

- What I Do When I Am Sick

- My Favorite Children's Story

Writing Projects

Individual Project: On a world map, trace your long trip. Indicate the number of miles (or kilometers) between stops on the trip. Write the time each part of the trip took, and mark the places you stopped. Then write several paragraphs about your long trip. Use some of the topics that follow:

- The First Part of My Trip

- A City Where My Plane Landed

- A Person I Met on My Trip

- The Plane I Travelled On

- What I Ate During My Trip

- The Best Part of My Trip

- The Worst Part of My Trip

- My Feelings During My Trip

Put your paragraphs into a booklet. Decorate the booklet with maps, with postcards from the cities you visited, and with photographs. Display the booklet in your class, and invite students from other classes to view it.

Group Project: Make a booklet advising students travelling abroad about the necessary arrangements they need to make. Use a check list for students like the one below to plan your project. Have each student in the class write about such arrangements in their own countries. Interview several students NOT in your class about arrangements that need to be made in other countries. Illustrate the booklet with the necessary forms and diagrams that will help students prepare for study abroad. Present the booklet to the foreign student advisor to help him or her counsel study-abroad students.

CHECKLIST FOR STUDENTS TRAVELLING ABROAD

3 months before the departure date:
    go to the embassy   _____
    get visa   _____
    _____   _____

2 months before the departure date:
    get papers   _____
    get academic transcripts   _____
    _____   _____

1 month before the departure date:
    _____   _____
    _____   _____

2 weeks before the departure date:
    _____   _____
    _____   _____

1 week before the departure date:
    _____   _____
    _____   _____

6

First Impressions, First Problems

The Airport

When I arrived at John F. Kennedy Airport in New York, I was really surprised because it was so big. First, the airport is divided into many small airports, one for each airline (like TWA and United and American Airlines). The gates for all the flights are very extensive, but the information about flights is hung on the walls, so I did not become lost. Finally, I found where to pick up my luggage. Then I went outside the airport because I had to travel to another airport to catch my next plane. I saw many parking lots, high buildings, and very wide roads, and I saw a lot of vans that transport people and their luggage from airport to airport. Above me, many planes were taking off and landing. There were so many that I couldn't count them; if I had been in my country, I would have said that they were birds, not planes. The noise from all these planes was unbelievable, but I thought it was wonderful.

Safouen Ben Brahim
Tunisia

ADJECTIVES AND ADVERBS

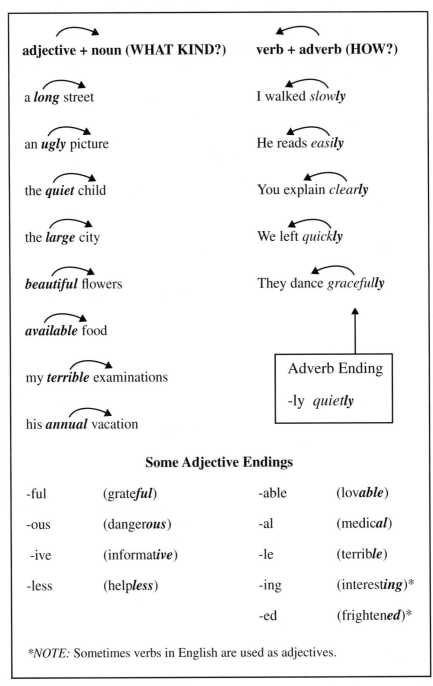

adjective + noun (WHAT KIND?)

a *long* street

an *ugly* picture

the *quiet* child

the *large* city

beautiful flowers

available food

my *terrible* examinations

his *annual* vacation

verb + adverb (HOW?)

I walked *slowly*

He reads *easily*

You explain *clearly*

We left *quickly*

They dance *gracefully*

Adverb Ending

-ly *quietly*

Some Adjective Endings

-ful	(grate*ful*)	-able	(lov*able*)
-ous	(danger*ous*)	-al	(medic*al*)
-ive	(informat*ive*)	-le	(terrib*le*)
-less	(help*less*)	-ing	(interest*ing*)*
		-ed	(frighten*ed*)*

NOTE: Sometimes verbs in English are used as adjectives.

ADJECTIVES AND ADVERBS (Continued)

Adjective	**Adverb**
He is a *careful* driver.	He drives *carefully*.
They are *quick* learners.	They learn *quickly*.

Exceptions

He is a ***FAST*** runner.	He runs ***FAST***.
They ate ***HARD*** candy.	They worked ***HARD***.

	Verb	**+ Adverb**	**+ Adjective**
She	is	real*ly*	youth*ful*.
Faizah	was	especial*ly*	surpris*ed*.
Masako	seems	**very**	humor*ous*.

Golden-Thread Clothes

Desire not golden-thread clothes.
Rather, enjoy your youth.
Good flowers are worth picking,
so go ahead and pick.
Don't wait until the flowers are gone,
and you can only pick the stem.

translated by
Prayat Laopropassone
Thailand

Exercise 6A

*Individually, or with a partner, look at the following adjectives. Cross out (**X**) the adjectives that do not fit with the nouns; the first **X** is done for you.*

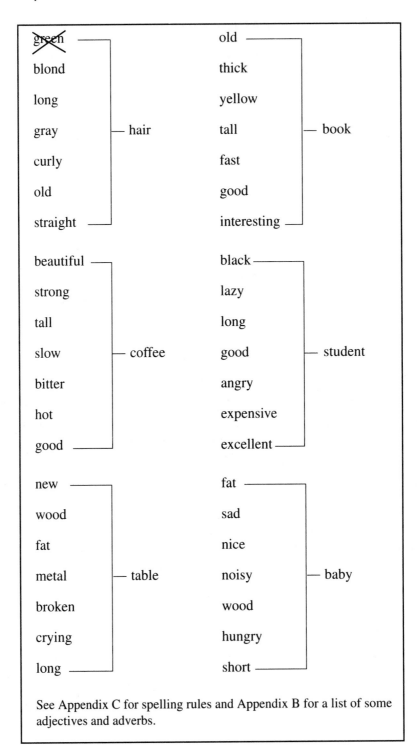

~~green~~			old	
blond			thick	
long			yellow	
gray	— hair		tall	— book
curly			fast	
old			good	
straight			interesting	

beautiful			black	
strong			lazy	
tall			long	
slow	— coffee		good	— student
bitter			angry	
hot			expensive	
good			excellent	

new			fat	
wood			sad	
fat			nice	
metal	— table		noisy	— baby
broken			wood	
crying			hungry	
long			short	

See Appendix C for spelling rules and Appendix B for a list of some adjectives and adverbs.

Exercise 6B

Write adjectives in the blanks that describe the following nouns. Then share your list with the lists of a small group of your classmates.

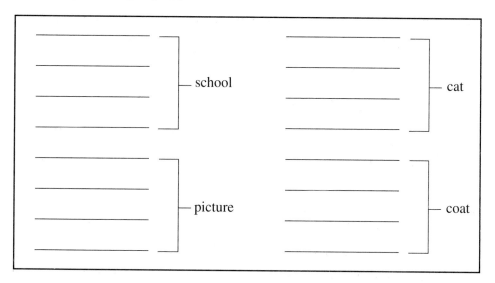

A Very *Pleasant* Surprise

When I first came to the U.S., the street where I lived surprised me because it was [very] clean and nice. On my first night in Santa Barbara, I went for a long walk around the neighborhood, and I did not see a single piece of paper or even a small piece of trash on the quiet street. In front of almost every house there were [many] beautiful flowers, and their smell, combined with the fresh air, followed me everywhere I went. I felt like I was in the country. Soft music escaped pleasantly from the house at the end of the street, so the sound of the darkness was like an endless song. In the large city where I grew up, there was an ugly pile of trash every two or three blocks. I could smell the garbage from my doorstep, and I could hear noisy car engines and motorcycles all day and all night. My neighbors argued [loudly] and [endlessly]. Because I expected the U.S. to be like my own country, I was [very] surprised when I saw the elegant street in my new neighborhood.

Mai Anh Tran
Vietnam

Exercise 6C

With a partner, read the poem that follows. Underline the adjectives and ⟨circle⟩ the adverbs in the poem. Then discuss the poem with your partner or with a small group of classmates.

- What is the poem about?

- What do you not understand?

- What do you like about it?

- What is confusing about the poem?

Lionrise

Glowing softly,
the giant yellow head
lifts itself from the cold ground.
The golden streamers
shimmer softly
and settle quietly into place.
Shading its face
with a fluffy orange paw
(which just happened to be drifting by)
it yawns discreetly,
closing lighted eyes
for only a moment,
enjoying one last sigh of darkness.
Flexing sleepy muscles
it climbs to its feet
and swishes its tail,
creating a small whirlwind
that gradually separates
into hundreds of individual breezes
that drift gently off
and disappear into the crisp morning air.
A brilliant eye
scans the blue savannah
and the crystal mountains
over which it must journey
before the day is over.
Beaming warmly down
on the awakening world,
it sets supple limbs in motion
and pads quietly off
toward the western horizon.

E. Shelley Reid
United States

Exercise 6D

With a small group of classmates, read the following paragraphs. Then do the exercises that follow each paragraph.

I

Strange Things

Moving from my country to continue my graduate study in the United States was a good chance for me. But when I first came to the U.S. I was very unhappy because I encountered many strange things. The strange people were especially surprising. I found that nobody spoke my language, and everybody wore funny clothes. So people for me were as different as the fingers on my hand. Another strange thing was the terrible food. For example, most American food contains at least a derivative of pork, but pork is forbidden by my religion. The third strange thing was the changeable weather. A single day could have a warm morning, a cold afternoon, and a thunderstorm! I was not used to living in such a changeable climate and different living conditions, so I was unhappy.

Khalid Al-Sawaf
Saudi Arabia

1. Underline at least 5 adjectives in the paragraph.
2. Circle 2 adverbs.
3. Put boxes around , and , , but or , so that joins two clauses.
4. What questions could you ask Khalid about this paragraph? What other paragraphs could Khalid write?

II

Indifferent Time

I cannot forget the day I left my country to go to the United States.

It _____ a bad day! I _____ very sad about leaving my family and
   be   **feel**

my friends. I _____ time to stop so I could always stay with them. But
              want

time was indifferent. The airplane was waiting for me. It was even on time.

My body felt tight because I didn't want to leave my home.

I _____ my family and my good friends through the tears which ran
  see

down my cheeks, although I did not want to cry. I _____ "Is this the
think
last time I'll see them? What will happen to me when I leave my family?"

I held my father, my mother, my brothers, my sisters, and all my friends.

Then I _____ goodbye. Now I have been living in California for nearly
say
three years, but pictures of my family and friends often rise in my mind. I

miss them very much.

Suong Ngoe Le
Vietnam

1. Write the past tense form of the verbs in the spaces.
2. (Circle) 3 adverbs and 3 adjectives.
3. What does the title, "Indifferent Time," mean?
4. Why was Suong worried about leaving her family? Have you had a similar experience?

> If you want to have an average living,
> you must have the habit of saving.
> If you want to be very rich,
> you must be very lucky.
>
> translated by
Man-Chiu Lu
Malaysia

Exercise 6E

With a partner, read the following paragraphs. Then do the exercises that follow each paragraph.

I

Traffic

One of the most important things that surprised me in the U.S.A. is the attention paid to traffic safety. The government _____ streets and highways carefully, so they _____ usually wide and divided. On both sides of the wide streets, there are large traffic signs which control the flow of heavy traffic on the roads. The signs with the speed limits and the traffic rules _____ fluorescent paint, so they can be seen easily at night. In addition, the citizens participate in traffic safety by obeying the laws. They always _____ when the signs say stop, and they are careful at every moment. They do not park their cars wherever they want, and they do not throw trash in the streets. Besides that, the policemen _____ to fix stalled cars, so the flow of traffic continues perfectly. All of these arrangements gave me a nice picture about the traffic in the U.S.A.

VERBS: be   have   help   plan   stop

Ivan Hernandez
Venezuela

1. Write the correct present tense verbs in the blanks. Use each verb on the list only once.
2. Underline at least 5 adjectives. Circle 4 adverbs.
3. Why is the title of this paragraph "Traffic"?
4. What do you remember about the paragraph?

II

Happiness

During my first weeks in the U.S., I _____ happiness. Before I _____ to the U.S. I was on the staff of a fabric company, and I _____ in a busy office. It seemed that I was on a battlefield. Of course, in those days, I did not notice the terrible environment because I was used to the atmosphere. Fortunately, I did not know there was a happy and gentle town like Lawrence, Kansas. When I arrived in Lawrence, I was very surprised at the beauty of the town, the quiet atmosphere, and the kindness of the people. I had had some impressions about America, and they _____ negative. However, the happiness that I found in Lawrence _____ my negative impressions. I was charmed by the town and the people, and I was really glad that I had made a good decision about the city where I would study in America. My great happiness, however, was that I found a beautiful and peaceful town which was quite different from my office. I love my town in Japan, and I also love my new hometown in America.

VERBS: be   change   come   find   work

Kimimasa Abe
Japan

1. Write the correct past tense verbs in the blanks. Use each verb on the list only once.

2. <u>Underline</u> at least 8 adjectives in the paragraph, and (circle) 3 adverbs.

3. What surprised Kimimasa?

4. What is the main idea in this paragraph? Discuss this question with your partner.

III

_____

   Dogs are treated differently in the United States than in my home country, Saudi Arabia. In my country, people treat dogs the same as they treat any animal. They do not like dogs. * Dogs are not allowed to enter houses. If a large number of dogs gather together in a neighborhood, people try to get rid of them. Dogs usually live around garbage areas. * People think they are dirty animals. If, by any chance, a dog touches a person's clothes, that person needs to wash his clothes immediately. But in the U.S., the situation is completely different. Here, dogs are considered as pets. People like them, and they are very proud of their dogs. Dogs live in houses with people. They sit on the sofas or even on the beds. They have special food, special clothes, and even special hospitals! Moreover, in the U.S., I have seen some people kiss their dogs. It was really a shock for me!

Mahamoud Wali
Saudi Arabia

1. <u>Underline</u> 3 adjectives, and (circle) 4 adverbs in the paragraph.

2. Join two clauses where you see the asterisk (*) with | , and | or | , so | .

3. Write a title for the paragraph.

4. Why was Mahamoud shocked? Discuss this question with your partner.

> If water could go uphill, the frog would sing, too.
>
> translated by
> *Keyvan Karbassiyon*
> Iran

Writing Assignment

Write a paragraph about a surprising problem you encountered in a new place or a new situation. Describe how you solved the problem. Use adjectives to describe the situation and your feelings.

1. Answer some of the following questions to plan the paragraph.

   - What was the problem?

   - What did you expect?

   - What was different from your expectations?

   - What did you discover?

   - What was similar to your expectations?

   - How did you feel about the problem? Happy? Anxious? Angry? Sad? Frustrated? WHY?

   - What did you do first?

   - Then what did you do?

   - Finally, what happened?

2. Exchange paragraphs with a classmate. Read the paragraph.

   A. Underline the adjectives, and circle the adverbs.

   B. Put parentheses ( ) around the prepositional phrases.

   C. What other paragraphs could your classmate write?

3. Ask your classmate questions about his/her paragraph.

4. Now, reread your paragraph.

   A. Answer your classmate's questions about your paragraph.

   B. What other changes can you make so that your paragraph will be better?

5. Rewrite your paragraph.

SPECIAL VERBS: SEE, HEAR, SAY, TELL

I *see [saw]* the airplane flying overhead. (Briefly)

I *look* (*at*) *[looked* (*at*)*]* my visa. (Carefully)

I *hear [heard]* the airplane flying overhead. (Briefly)

I *listen* (*to*) *[listened* (*to*)*]* the stereo. (Carefully)

They *say* (*that*) *[said* (*that*)*]* they were homesick.

They *tell* (me, my friend) (*that*) they are homesick.

They *told* (me, my friend) (*that*) they were homesick.

Mosquitos!

I HEARD a lot of stories about the U.S. back in my country, Nigeria. One person SAID THAT there were no mosquitos or insects in the United States because of the cold climate. However, five days after my arrival in Macomb, Illinois, I SAW mosquitos outside our living room door. I was saying goodbye to some visitors when I first SAW the mosquitos. Then I LOOKED AT my son, and I SAW a mosquito on his arm. I grabbed his arm, and I killed the mosquito. Suddenly I HEARD my little daughter cry because another mosquito had bitten her. I rushed to her and killed the mosquito, and blood gushed out on my palms. My daughter's hand was a bit swollen the following day. So I TOLD my husband THAT it was not true there were not mosquitos in the U.S., and I wondered why I had LISTENED TO the stories in Nigeria.

Margaret A. Obaja
Nigeria

Exercise 6F

With a small group of classmates, read the following paragraphs. Then do the exercises that follow each paragraph.

I

Homesickness

When I first came to the U.S., I was very homesick. I married my husband one week before we came here. * I left my wonderful family for the first time. Every day my husband went to the university. * I stayed in the apartment. I cleaned the room and our clothes. * Then I thought about my family and my good friends. I tried to listen to the radio. * I could not understand the language. I watched television. * I did not understand. Then I cried. * I spent many hours looking at beautiful photographs of my family. For two months I stayed in that terrible apartment. I did not go to the university or to the supermarket. I did not have any friends. I stayed in my apartment. * I cried when I remembered my friends.

Hussa Al-Hitmi
Qatar

1. <u>Underline</u> the "special verbs": <u>see, listen to, watch, look at.</u>
2. Circle 2 adverbs in the paragraph.
3. Join two clauses where you see the asterisks (*) with `, and` or `, but`.
4. Why was Hussa so unhappy? What advice could you give her to make her experience better?

II

Machines

One thing that really amazed me when I first _____ in the United States was the large number of things one can get from coin-operated machines. During my first hours in the United States, I was able to buy many things without making contact with a human being. All I _____ was a few coins in my hand. For example, I saw machines all around the airport. I _____ a can of Coke, a candy bar, and a pack of gum because I was very hungry. Later, at my hotel, I saw more machines, so I bought some chips and a newspaper, and I put coins in the television to watch a movie. When I told my friends about my unusual experiences, they laughed. Then they _____ me machines that sold postage stamps and air letters, even when the post office _____ closed. For entertainment, I _____ I could use coins to play video games or listen to the music of my choice on juke boxes in restaurants. Now, when I put coins into a machine to do my laundry, I also buy cigarettes and coffee from machines in the laundromat. I never go anywhere without a handful of coins!

VERBS: arrive   be   buy   find   need   show

Leung Iai
Singapore

1. Write the past tense verbs in the blanks. Use each verb on the list only once.
2. <u>Underline</u> the "special verbs"; <u>see, listen, tell</u>.
3. Circle 2 adjectives and 2 adverbs in the paragraph.
4. Look again at the student paragraphs about first impressions and first problems in this chapter. Which paragraph did you like most? Why? Discuss your answer with your classmates.

III

Learning the Eurorail

Last summer my brother Doug and I _____ 14 days travelling all around Europe. For those two weeks we _____ a Eurorail pass that gave us unlimited travel on the elaborate European railroad system. Since we come from a background that did not include riding trains, we had many problems. At first, when we decided to visit one of Doug's friends in northern Germany, we had trouble figuring out which train to take. We studied the train timetable, selected the train we thought we wanted, got aboard, and quickly settled down in one of the empty cabins. However, thirty minutes later, the conductor came by and asked (we think) where we were going. When we replied, she _____ signaling and trying to tell us that we had missed our stop, and that we were going to Switzerland. We looked at each other. * Then we laughed and started to plan what we would do in Switzerland. Then the conductor _____ back. * This time she _____ a young lady who spoke a little English with her. The lady explained that we were in the wrong cabin, and that we needed to go three cars toward the front—we hadn't missed our stop after all! As we began looking for another seat, we passed two American girls and one American guy, so we spent the remainder of the night talking with them. They invited us to come to Amsterdam with them. * We accepted, going to a completely different place than we had planned.

VERBS: begin   buy   come   spend   bring

Richard Powell
United States

1. Write the past tense verbs in the blanks. Use each verb on the list only once.

2. Join two clauses where you see the asterisks (*) with ⟨ , and ⟩.

3. ⟨Circle⟩ 2 adjectives and 2 adverbs in the paragraph.

4. What questions could you ask Richard about his paragraph? How could he make his paragraph more interesting?

Nothing can cool off your itches like your own fingernails.

translated by
Adel Salamah
Iran

Interview

Interview someone NOT in your class about:

A. his or her first impression of a new situation or a new place *OR*

B. his or her most surprising problem in a new situation or a new place.

1. Ask some of the questions on page 151 to collect information. Then plan a paragraph about your friend's feelings or experiences. In the paragraph, use such expressions as:

> he said that...
> she told me that...

2. As you write your paragraph, do the following:

A. Use adjectives and adverbs in the paragraph.

B. In some sentences, use , and , , but or , so to join two clauses.

3. Exchange paragraphs with a classmate. Read your partner's paragraph.

A. Underline the special verbs: say, tell.

B. Circle the adjectives and the adverbs.

C. Put boxes around two clauses that are joined by , and , , but or , so .

D. What questions could you ask your classmate about the paragraph?

4. Now, reread your paragraph.

A. Show your paragraph to the friend you interviewed. Does your friend have any suggestions for improving your paragraph?

B. Think about the questions your partner asked you about your paragraph. Do you need to talk with your friend in order to collect more information?

C. What changes can you make in your paragraph to make it more interesting?

5. Rewrite your paragraph and share it with a partner in your class.

SPECIAL ADVERBS: TOO AND VERY

> The weather was *very* cold, but I could still go outside.
>
> (*possible* but difficult)
>
> The weather was *too* cold, so I could <u>not</u> go outside.
>
> (negative, *impossible*)

Culture Shock

When a person travels from his home country to another one, he will sometimes feel VERY uncomfortable. This is called "culture shock." One thing that shocked me when I came to the States was the "tip" or "tax." For example, I entered the U.S. in San Francisco, and I spent one night in a hotel that cost $35 per night. The next morning I prepared $35 to pay my bill. I was VERY surprised when the clerk asked for a little more than $35. I thought he was making me pay <u>TOO</u> much. However, he told me that the additional money was for tax. He also said that I must leave a 10%–15% tip. Thus I paid more than I was prepared to pay. I have learned that most merchandise in the U.S. is taxed. Even when I buy food at the market, the clerk charges about 5% of the total receipt. Also, whenever I go to a restaurant, I leave a tip at my place for 15% of the bill. Although there are no tips or taxes in China, I am learning about the U.S. culture.

Jin Lu
China (P.R.C.)

Exercise 6G

With a small group of classmates, read the following paragraphs. Then do the exercises that follow each paragraph.

I

Housing

When I left Korea for my first trip abroad, I expected many things. But I did not know that finding an apartment would be so frustrating. When I arrived, my friend took me to the university housing office. The secretary said, "It's very difficult to give you university housing at this moment—maybe in three months." I felt very anxious, but my friend helped me look in the newspaper "want ads." We went to look at two or three apartments, but there was a problem. <u>I had to sign a contract for a year.</u> Therefore, I would not be able to move to university housing in three months. My friends tried to encourage me, but I could not think about anything. <u>I was very worried about the problem.</u> I was living in a hotel, and I was spending too much money. <u>Finally, I found an apartment at Prospect Plaza.</u> <u>The rooms in the apartment were very clean.</u> The manager gave me a checklist about the apartment, and he told me to check any problems in the apartment. Then I signed a three-month contract, and my friend helped me move my luggage into the apartment.

Jong-Hub Park
Korea

1. <u>Underline</u> the special adverbs: <u>too</u> and <u>very.</u> What does each mean in the paragraph?

2. Make the <u>underlined</u> sentences negative.

3. Put boxes around the ⬛, and ⬛ or ⬛, but ⬛ that joins two clauses.

4. Why was finding an apartment frustrating for Park? Discuss your answer with your group.

II

Cooking

Probably the worst experience I _____ during my life in the U.S. was in the kitchen: cooking, washing dishes, shopping, etc. Of course, I first experienced life in restaurants, but after only two weeks I _____ so broke that I did not want to think more about eating in restaurants. Besides the fact that the restaurants cost too much, I was never able to understand the menus, unless they came with some nice pictures. Therefore, I _____ to start my kitchen "studies." At the beginning, I _____ really humiliated since I was still thinking like I did at home. I thought that the kitchen was the kind of job only for women. What a silly idea! Then I was very ashamed of myself for not being able to do the simple kitchen work. I still remember my first dinner, if it could be called dinner. It was boiled, salted rice with hard chicken. I _____ it all because I was really hungry, and also I did not want to demonstrate my incompetence to my roommate.

VERBS: be   decide   eat   feel   have

Herve John Raymond
Haiti

1. Write the correct past tense verbs in the blanks. Use each verb on the list only once.

2. <u>Underline</u> the special adverbs: <u>too</u> and <u>very.</u> What does each mean in the paragraph?

3. (Circle) three verbs + adjectives of feeling in the paragraph.

4. Why did Herve feel humiliated? Discuss your answer with your group.

III

Distressing Complexities

I was very distressed by the complexity of daily life in the first two months after I arrived in the U.S. For example, the complex procedures to see a doctor are very different from those in my country. In the U.S., I found that I could not go to see a doctor immediately if I felt sick because I needed to make an appointment first. I always had to wait a few days to get into his schedule. For example, two weeks after I arrived, I called a doctor's office to make an appointment for a fungus infection on my foot. The nurse told me that the schedule was full. Two days later the infection was worse, and it hurt terribly. After the doctor made his diagnosis, he gave me a prescription. However, I needed to go to the pharmacy to fill it instead of getting the medicine directly from the doctor. Finally, when I paid the doctor's bill, the nurse asked me if I had insurance. We do not think of medical insurance when we go to the doctor in my country, but we certainly must in the U.S. because without insurance, medical expenses are too great. In my country this entire experience would only have taken one day, but in the U.S. it took more than two weeks to solve the problem of my infected foot.

Chia-Chu Dorland
Taiwan (R.O.C.)

1. Underline the special adverbs: too and very. What does each mean in the paragraph?

2. Circle at least two adjectives and two adverbs.

3. Put parentheses ( ) around the pronouns in the paragraph. Identify the subject pronouns (S) and the object pronouns (O).

4. Have you had a similar experience? Discuss similar experiences with your group.

> Learning is like a boat going upstream:
> if one does not row hard enough,
> the boat will definitely go down the stream.
>
> translated by
> *Man-Chiu Lu*
> Malaysia

Writing Assignment

You have just arrived in the United States, and you are looking for an apartment. Read the newspaper "want ads" that follow. Then write a paragraph to a friend. Describe how you found an apartment.

1. With a partner or a small group, study the "want ads" below. Then decide what kind of apartment you want.

708 Rentals to share

SHARE newly remodeled 2-bdrm apt with male. Fully furnished except bdrm, $150/month, ½ utilities. 224-9214.

SHARE QUIET 3 bdrm, 1 mile CSU, fenced, laundry, $175 plus ⅓ utilities. 493-3180 after 5pm

SHARE 2 bdrm apt., fireplace, cheap utilities, new washer/dryer! $207.50/deposit. 224-5525.

TO SHARE 3 bdrm newer house, close to CSU, fireplace, gas grill, fenced yard, nice area, $150/month. 224-4340/484-6291

TO SHARE 4-bdrm house. $155/month. plus utilities. Clean and responsible persons need only inquire. Rob 482-2956.

710 Rooms to rent

ABDICATE HIGH RENT. Private room, cozy. 510 S Howes. $100 per mo 1-669-6754 collect.

AVAILABLE IN home, Jan. 15. Near Fashion Mall and bus routes. Washer/dryer, quiet. $165 plus utilities. 223-0097.

FURNISHED sleeping room $112/mo utilities paid. Refrigerator space available. 221-5888
MAIL CREEK PROPERITES

ROOM FOR NON-SMOKER
Kitchen privleges.
$175 Plus deposit. 482-1285

ROOMY SUITE. Female, non-smoker, fireplace, rent for horse care. $235/$195. 493-8220.

712 Furnished apartments

A BASEMENT 2 BDRM, very clean, close to CSU, $275. Bunton Realty, 221-1600 or 221-3843.

ACROSS FROM NEW HOLIDAY INN! Studios, 1 and 2 bdrms, all utilities paid. $245, $300, $360
304 W Prospect, 482-9513

A QUIET 2 BDRM BASEMENT, near the malls. Adults only. Many extras. Call 221-1788.

AVAILABLE. 2 bdrm, very clean, near Moby Gym, pet ok, $350. Bunton Realty, 221-1600 or 221-3843.

BEST DEALS in town 1-bdrm $225 2/3 bills paid garage. Renter's Guide 484-1380 Fee C-1

BUFFET with kitchenette, $185/month includes utilities. Horsetooth area. 226-2934

CAMBRIDGE HOUSE Apts. has 2 bdrm apts. with free cable tv, indoor pool and clubhouse. Right across from CSU, 1113 W. Plum. 484-7756.

CLEAN 1-bdrm, available Jan 1. $275 Plus utilities. No pets. 915 James Court. 1-499-5709

WON'T LAST. Studio and 2 bdrm apartments, close to CSU. Pool, furnished or unfurnished. $225-$395. 775 W. Lake, call Russ. 484-1446 1-5 PM or Foxfire Property Management, 224-9207, No Fee.

KITCHENETTES, special winter rates. TV, phone, laundry, weekly, monthly. Plainsman Motel, 482-9744, 1310 N. College.

LARGE BRIGHT 1 bdrm basement apt. Share kitchen with one other. City Park area. $200, share utilities. 493-4543.

LARGE 1 BDRM, all utilities paid except electric, next to campus, $300 a month. 224-3616.

NICE 1-bdrm close to CSU. $275. 919 James Court. Anderson CO 484-5115

ONE-EXTRA large bdrm in 4-plex. Heat/water/sewer/trash paid, no pets. $300. Anderson Company 484-5115

QUIET 2 BDRM basement apartment, 1 block from campus, no smokers, or pets $250 a month plus utilities. Available Feb. 1. Call 493-9031.

SCOTCH PINES EAST

Furnished studio, all appliances plus washer/dryer, fireplace, outdoor pool, clubhouse, tennis courts, adult area, 3 or 6 month lease, $300 plus utilities. 915 East Drake Road, 223-4038

HEATHERIDGE! 2 bdrm, 1½ baths, laundry, amenities. No pets. $395. Mountain-N-Plains, 221-2361, 8-5. Sat. 9-12. No Fee.

HEAT PAID, 1-bdrm. 610 Stover, No 3. Cat OK. Courtyard, $260. 221-0763; 493-5290 after 5pm

What kind of apartment I need: _____

_____

_____

2. Decide what information you want to use in your paragraph by collecting the following information.

Finding an Apartment

Information I need to know *before* I begin looking: _____

_____

_____

_____

Questions I need to ask the apartment manager: _____

_____

_____

_____

3. As you write your paragraph, do the following:

   A. Use adjectives and adverbs in your paragraph.

   B. Use time connectors and present tense verbs.

The current will take any shrimp that is not awake.

translated by
Douglas Chang
Ecuador

PRESENT CONTINUOUS VERBS
(RIGHT NOW)*

TO BE + VERB + -ING

I am cooking dinner. (right now)

He *is watching* television. (right now)

She *is listening* to the radio. (right now)

It *is snowing* (right now)

You are talking on the telephone. (right now)

We *are looking* at an apartment. (right now)

They *are running* (right now)

*See Appendix D for spelling rules.

Adjustments

Last week, my husband Armando and I arrived in Mexico City. This week I <u>AM</u> <u>ADJUSTING</u> to my new life, but I <u>AM</u> <u>HAVING</u> some problems. First, I do not know the city, so I must depend on Armando's friends to help me. I was very independent when I lived in the U.S., so this is difficult for me. Second, I <u>AM</u> not <u>WORKING</u> because we will be moving to Aguascalientes in two months. Therefore, I <u>AM</u> <u>SPENDING</u> my time reading, cooking, and washing and ironing Armando's shirts. Finally, we <u>ARE</u> <u>LIVING</u> with a family. The man <u>IS</u> <u>WORKING</u> in the same company as Armando. The people are very nice, but the situation does have some disadvantages. So although we are not established in a normal way of life, we will soon move to a new town and our own apartment.

Susan Yamine Valencia
United States

Exercise 6H

With a partner, read the following paragraphs. Then do the exercises that follow each paragraph.

I

Arrival in Jeddah

Jeddah is not what I expected. I was surprised, for example, that English is

the official business language, so I _____ trouble with my day-to-
be + not + have
day activities. I _____ in a nice two-bedroom home on the
be + live
company compound. The company _____ excellent support
be + provide
activities like a gymnasium, scuba diving, and tennis courts. I

_____ a university course in computer science and a class in
be + take
Arabic, so I am very busy. Besides my life in the compound, there is quite a lot to

do in the city itself. Tonight I _____ to see one of the theatre
be + go
groups perform, and I have also been to the opera and to the square dance club. In

short, I _____ life here to be quite enjoyable.
be + find

Doug Ellis
United States

1. Write the correct present continuous verb in the blanks.
2. Put boxes around the ⌐ , and ⌐ or ⌐ , so ⌐ that joins two clauses.
3. ⟨Circle⟩ 4 adjectives and 1 adverb in the paragraph.
4. What is the main idea in this paragraph? Discuss your answer with your partner.

II

Cusco's Street Sounds

One of the most surprising things about Cusco, Peru, is the street

sounds. Right now I _____ to men calling for bottles and the
be + listen
scissor sharpeners with their continual special call. Dozens of horns

_____ and the cars are very noisy. I don't think they have any
be + honk
mufflers at all. The street vendors _____ to the passersby, and
be + shout
the beggars _____ to the tourists. Because it is a weekend,
be + call
there is also music in the street, and people _____ to celebrate
be + dance
a feast day. All of those sounds _____ together into a unique
be + blend
concert, and I am glad that I am here to hear it.

Selma Myers
United States

1. Write the correct present continuous verbs in the blanks.
2. Put boxes around ⌐ , and ⌐ that joins two clauses.
3. Put parentheses ( ) around 5 prepositional phrases.
4. Have you had a similar experience? Discuss your answer with your partner.

Writing Assignment

Choose a classmate. Write a paragraph about that classmate. Describe what he or she is doing RIGHT NOW. Use present continuous verbs. Use adjectives and adverbs.

1. Answer some of the following questions.

    • What is he or she wearing?

    • What is he or she doing?

        • Five seconds later: Now?

        • Ten seconds later: Now?

        • Thirty seconds later: Now?

    • What do you suppose he or she is thinking about?

2. Write the paragraph.

3. Exchange paragraphs with that classmate. Read your partner's paragraph.

    A. <u>Underline</u> the present continuous verbs.

    B. Ⓒircle the adjectives.

    C. Put a box around the ⟨ , and ⟩ , ⟨ , but ⟩ or ⟨ , so ⟩ that joins two clauses.

    D. Is the description of you written by your classmate accurate? Discuss your answer with your partner.

PAST CONTINUOUS VERBS (LAST WEEK, YESTERDAY)*

BE + VERB + -ING

I *was visiting* my friend.   (yesterday)

He *was planning* his trip.   (last week)

She *was having* some problems.   (last month)

It *was raining* very hard.   (last April)

You *were living* with your friend.   (last year)

We *were walking* to the train station.   (yesterday)

They *were working* together.   (last Tuesday)

*See Appendix D for spelling rules

Images of Cameroon

Last week Mr. Wanji invited Helen and me over for dinner and to watch a soccer match on television. As we arrived, the sun <u>WAS STRIKING</u> a bank of clouds from behind, and they were illuminated in a multitude of pastel colors: pink, purple, yellow, blue, and green. We were greeted by Mr. Wanji and his wife, who introduced us to the other dinner guests. Before we began eating, one of the young women brought around a large bowl of water, a cake of soap, and a towel. We watched as the other guests <u>WERE WASHING</u> their hands, and then we washed ours. Then Mr. Doumbé, a Catholic, gave a prayer before the meal. The first dinner course consisted of a large platter of shredded purple and green cabbage, sliced green peppers, and tomatoes surrounding by slices of avocado. Next we were served boiled plantains and goat, followed by chicken fried in palm oil, with hot pepper sauce for those who wished it, and then papaya for dessert. During dinner, a German man who <u>WAS LIVING</u> in Cameroon noted sadly that books were so difficult to obtain—that one could find more books about Cameroon in Munich or Paris than in Yaoundé.

Mary Lee Scott
United States

There are two kinds of death:
one is heavier than the mountain,
while the other is lighter than fur.

translated by
John Shyh-Yuan Wang
China (P.R.C.)

Exercise 6I

With a partner or a small group of classmates, read the following paragraphs. Then do the exercises that follow each paragraph.

I

First Impressions of Mali

My first impression of Mali is that the people are wonderful. Right now,

my husband and I _____ in a large private room in a family home
be + live
in Bamako. The family is very aware of our needs and our differences. Of course,

they are amazed that we are incompetent at doing simple things, but they

_____ us to learn. For example, this morning I
     be + help
_____ to wash clothes in a bucket and to use my left hand as a
     be + learn
washboard. Yesterday I tried to pound millet with a mortar and pestle, and I watched

the woman in the family as she _____ dried nuts. Shopping for
                 be + shell
food is another lesson I _____ today. Most fresh food is sold in
           be + practice
open markets, and I must bargain in both French and Bambara. Fortunately, the

Malians accept my feeble attempts to speak their language, and slowly

I _____ my French.
     be + improve

Linda Stratton
United States

1. Write the correct present continuous AND past continuous verbs in the blanks. How do you know which tense to use? Discuss your answer with your partner or your small group of classmates.

2. (Circle) two adjectives in the paragraph.

3. Put parentheses ( ) around five prepositional phrases.

4. Have you had a similar experience? Discus your answer with your partner or your small group of classmates.

II

Impressions Upon Returning Home

After spending a year in France, my family and I returned to the United

States for a month's visit. We were surprised to find how different and strange the

United States had become. As we _____ the airport, we noticed
           be + leave
how much bigger everything seemed. The cars, the highways, and the potholes were

huge! Life also seemed so much faster. Everyone _____
                              be + hurry

somewhere, and no one looked very happy. We _____ too, trying
be + hurry
to shop, to see the dentist and doctor, and to visit friends. For us, the most frustrating

thing was the lack of public transportation. We had to drive our car everywhere, and

American drivers are not as courteous as we had thought! Of course, we enjoyed

American beef, American ice cream, and especially iced tea, but we were sad about

the filthy roadsides, the graffiti, and the ever-present television programs. As

we _____ to France, we all agreed that we would be much more
be + return
tolerant of our life in Paris!

Ruth Doré
United States

1. Write the correct past continuous verbs in the blanks.

2. (Circle) the pronouns in the paragraph, and identify them as subject pronouns (S) or object pronouns (O).

3. How is this paragraph different from the previous two paragraphs? Discuss your answer with your partner or with your group.

4. What ideas do you remember about the paragraph? Discuss these ideas with your partner or with your small group of classmates.

III

Reverse Culture Shock

I experienced reverse culture shock when I _____ Italy on
be + visit
holiday from Rumania last year. It was the day before Christmas, and I was on my

way to Italy. The previous week in Rumania had been particularly bad. It was bitter

cold, and only a few trolleys _____ because of an energy problem.
be + run
Crowds   of   people _____ into   the   street.   They

be + drift
_____ for transportation. The day before I left for Italy, a big

be + search

shipment of oranges came from Turkey, and as I _____ , I saw a
be + leave
line of frozen people that stretched for three city blocks.

Everyone _____ for Christmas oranges. The next night, as my
be + wait
bus _____ the border of Yugoslavia into Italy, the first little town
be + cross
was decorated with enough lights to support Bucharest for a couple of days. Carts

of fruit spilled out of store doorways into the night air. I was surprised to see bananas

and pineapples. All this fruit, and no one _____ it! Great
be + buy
carcasses of meat hung from the ceiling of a brightly lit butcher shop. The Christmas

lights densely lined the streets, and there was food everywhere. But suddenly I was

surprised to discover that I really wanted to go back to Bucharest where life was

stark and simple.

Marian Aitches
United States

1. Write the correct past continuous verbs in the blanks.
2. Put boxes around the ⎡ , and ⎤ that joins two clauses (at least three sentences).
3. What is the main idea of this paragraph? Discuss your answer with your partner.
4. Have you had a similar experience? Discuss your answer with your partner.

Never look for birds of this year in the nests of the last.

translated by
Vicki Miller
Spain

Writing Assignment

You are a student on a U.S. university campus, and you are surprised when you see the picture below in the university newspaper. With a partner, write ONE paragraph that <u>describes</u> the picture. In the paragraph, explain why this paragraph surprises you and your partner. Use present continuous verbs, and use adjectives and adverbs.

Bomar, a four-year-old, fifty-pound shepherd-husky dog, gets a ride from his owner, Jim Hoffman, a senior at Colorado State University. Hoffman said that Bomar enjoys riding this way and has done so for the past three years. The pair, traveling on Balsam Lane, were on their way to visit a friend. (Photo courtesy of *The Fort Collins Coloradoan* newspaper.)

1. Exchange paragraphs with another set of partners.

   A. Read the other partners' paragraph.

   B. <u>Underline</u> the present continuous verbs.

   C. (Circle) the adjectives.

   D. Put parentheses ( ) around the adverbs.

2. Discuss the two paragraphs. How could you and your partner make your paragraph more interesting?

3. With your partner, rewrite your paragraph.

   A. Make the changes you decide on.

   B. Use past tense verbs instead of present continuous.

Treading secretly,
rain falls between my hands,
knitting sorrow, lonely.
When the east wind comes,
I step within myself.

Van Tran
Vietnam

Writing Assignment

Translate a short poem from your language into English. <u>Underline</u> the adjectives and (circle) the adverbs in your translation. Then write a paragraph that describes the problems you had translating the poem. Did you have problems with

- vocabulary? What words?

- grammar? Which structures?

- verbs? In what ways?

- ideas? Why?

Exchange your translated poem and your paragraph with classmates in a small group. Read two to three poems and paragraphs. Discuss the poem you liked best with your groups. Then discuss problems you had translating the poem.

Other Writing Topics

- How My First Impressions of Someone Were Right (or Wrong)

- How My First Impressions of Something Were Right (or Wrong)

- One Thing About My Country That a Foreign Visitor Might Find Surprising (or Strange, or Frightening)

- How I Prepared Mentally for My Long Trip

Writing Projects

Individual Project: Translate several poems and sayings from your language. Make a booklet of these sayings. You might also include translations of several children's stories from your culture. Decorate the booklet with pictures and artwork. Present the booklet to the children's section of the public library.

Group Project: Make a booklet with paragraphs about culture shock. Use the paragraphs written by class members, and interview other students about their experiences with culture shock. Write paragraphs from those interviews, and include them in the booklet. Illustrate the booklet with drawings and cartoons.

Make copies of the booklet for the students who participated, and present a copy of the booklet to the Office of International Services, the International Education Department, or the foreign student advisor for use in their orientations and cross-cultural classes.

7

Adjustments and Solutions

Adjustments

My life in college was not simple at first because I had to adjust to two new changes. My first adjustment was in my school life. The studies were different from those in high school, so I had to learn new ways of studying. For example, I could not rely on a summary that the teacher gave after each lesson. Instead, I had to take notes while the teacher gave his lecture. Also, I had to learn to use a library. This was important because for most of my classes I needed to go to the library to do research. The second adjustment was to live on my own money. I had to manage my scholarship money for my expenses. Before college, I never lived far from my parents, and I did not have to pay rent. Thus, at first I had trouble budgeting my money. For example, some money had to be kept for transportation, and I had to pay for meals and rent. In addition to that, I had to buy clothing, and sometimes I needed money for entertainment. Now, I still study in college, but fortunately the adjustments are over.

Hamidou Berthé
Mali

> Worrying is a waste of time, and over a lifetime, worry will cost you years.
>
> Translated by
> *Pamela Liu*
> Taiwan (R.O C.)

INFINITIVE VERBS

TO + (root form of the verb)

(S)	(V)	Infinitive	Complement
I	learn*ed*	TO SPEAK	English.
He	expects	TO PASS	the TOEFL exam.
She	likes	TO READ	poetry.
It	was a good day	TO HAVE	a picnic.
You	promis*ed*	TO COME	to her wedding.
We	agree*d*	TO PLAY	the piano.
They	continue	TO TALK	on the telephone.

Negative Verbs and the Infinitive

(S)	(V)	Infinitive	Complement
I	*did not* learn*	TO SPEAK	English.
He	*does not* expect*	TO PASS	the TOEFL exam.
She	*does not* like*	TO READ	poetry.
It	*was not* a good day*	TO HAVE	a picnic.
You	*did not* promise*	TO COME	to her wedding.
We	*did not* agree*	TO PLAY	the piano.
They	*do not* continue*	TO TALK	on the telephone.

*The root form of the verb is used with the negative.

Eating in the U.S.A.

One of the most distressing parts of culture shock I experienced in the United States was eating. Starting from the very beginning, when I was on the airplane, I remember that everything I ate was sour. I [did not want] TO TOUCH any of the food the next time it was served. After I landed, I went to a restaurant for my dinner. The waitress gave me a menu, but I could not order properly because I [did not know] which food was which. The only dish that I knew was beef steak, so I ordered a steak. I thought that I was finished ordering, but the waitress surprised me by asking a series of questions. "Do you want it rare, medium, or well done?" After that, she asked me about different kinds of salad dressing, dessert, and drink. At that time, I was very confused. Even now. I still [do not know] what "Thousand Island dressing" is. I still cannot order a meal comfortably because I have TO MAKE so many decisions. In Taiwan, if I go to a restaurant, I only need TO TELL the waitress the name of the dish because each dish has fixed ingredients. I [do not need] TO ANSWER questions, and I [do not need] TO MAKE thousands of decisions. TO SOLVE this problem in the United States, I have learned TO COOK my own meals.

Tai-Whang Chow
Taiwan (R.O.C.)

Exercise 7A

Read the following paragraphs. Then do the exercises that follow each paragraph.

I

The Problems of Language

The main problem I had when I _____ in the United States was the language. Of course, I knew this would happen, and I expected it. I _____ to the United States to study English for a year, so I _____ the problems would be small. That was not true. I was not used to the accent people speak in this region, so I _____ a hard time understanding them. Also, the people _____ very quickly, and they did not pronounce some of the letters in the words. My friends _____ me that I would be able to understand the language better in a very short time—two or three weeks. Fortunately, they were correct. Now, after just one month, I understand much more, and I think, as my friends said, "It's just a matter of time."

VERBS: arrive   come   have   speak   tell   think

Marcus Henrique Tessler
Brazil

1. Write the correct past tense verbs in the blanks. Use each verb on the list only once.
2. Circle 2 infinitive verbs in the paragraph.
3. What did Marcus find frustrating about the U.S.?
4. Have you ever felt the same way? Discuss your ideas with your classmates.

II

University Procedures

I needed to understand the procedures of the university. * I was confused about information about "credits" and required classes. I did not understand the registration process. In addition, the university system in American universities is very free. * Choosing a correct program of study is difficult. Another problem was that the Admissions Office did not know the education system in my country, Belgium, so I had to explain my complete background. Fortunately, I found two good ways to solve my problems. First, the Foreign Student Office was very helpful. Two people there spoke my language, French. * They listened to my problems and answered my questions. They also talked to the Admissions Office, and then they directed me to my "academic advisor." She advised me about the registration procedure. Therefore, I was able to enroll easily for this semester's classes.

Veronica Lenders
Belgium

1. Underline 4 infinitive verbs.
2. Circle at least 2 adjectives and 2 adverbs.
3. Join two clauses with , and ,   , but   or   , so   where you see the asterisks (*).
4. What is the main idea in this paragraph? Discuss your ideas with your classmates.

III

Adjustment to Classes

I am adjusting to the new, exciting, and frightening method of study in the United States. In addition to the language, there are many differences in the ways of teaching and learning between my country and the United States. For example, in the United States, some classes are lectures, some are discussion, and some are presentations. The instructors often encourage the students to express their ideas, and the students do not hesitate to do that. Also, the students are eager to get more knowledge, and the library is an important tool in successful learning. In my country, on the other hand, most classes are lectures. The instructors tell the students all the information. The students listen carefully to the lecture, and they write down what the instructor says. Some instructors allow students to express their ideas, but most students are reluctant to do this because they are afraid of making a mistake. Finally, in Thailand students do not usually use the library. Now that I am studying in the United States, I have to learn to adjust to the new experiences. I am learning to use the library, and sometimes I raise my hand and express myself in class. When I began my classes, the adjustment was very difficult, but now it is easier.

Pang Suwanchinda
Thailand

1. (Circle) 8 infinitive verbs.

2. Underline 3 present continuous verbs.

3. What is Pang learning to do?

4. Have you had a similar experience? Discuss your answer with your classmates.

> In the sea of knowledge, diligence is the shore.
>
> translated by
> *Alice Lo*
> Hong Kong

Writing Assignment

You have invited a classmate to your apartment (or house or dormitory) for dinner. Draw a map that shows your friend how to get from your classroom to your home. Then exchange maps with that classmate. Use your classmate's map to write a paragraph about how to get from your classroom to your classmate's home.

1. Answer some of the questions below to plan your paragraph.

   • How far is it to your classmate's home?

   • How will you get to his or her home? (By car? By bus? By walking?)

   • When you leave your classroom building, what should you do first? (Turn right? Walk one block north? Drive two miles east?)

   • What street should you go to?

   • Then what should you do? After that? Then? Finally?

2. As you write your paragraph, do the following:

   A. Use time connectors in the paragraph.

   B. Use some infinitive verbs in your paragraph.

C. Use ⟦ , and ⟧, ⟦ , but ⟧ or ⟦ , so ⟧ to join clauses in your paragraph.

D. If necessary, ask your classmate questions about his or her map so that you can complete your paragraph.

3. Exchange paragraphs with your classmate:

A. Read your partner's paragraph.

B. Is it a correct description of how to get to your home? Discuss any suggestions for changes with your partner.

C. Underline any language errors you find in the paragraph, such as verb tense, pronouns, or spelling.

D. Discuss the errors with your classmate, and correct the errors.

4. Reread your paragraph. Make any changes that will improve your paragraph.

5. Rewrite your paragraph. Then share it with a small group of classmates.

6. As you read two or three of your classmates' paragraphs, decide which paragraph you like best. Discuss your answer with your group.

SPECIAL INFINITIVE VERBS

Have To, Need To, Want To			
(S)	**(V)**	**Infinitive**	**Complement**
I	[have	TO] GO	to the supermarket.
I	[had	TO] GO	to the supermarket.
He	[needs	TO] STUDY	for the test.
She	[needed	TO] STUDY	for the test.
We	[want	TO] DRIVE	the new car.
They	[wanted	TO] DRIVE	the new car.

SPECIAL INFINITIVE VERBS (continued)

Negative Special Infinitive Verbs*				
I	*do not*	[have	TO] GO	to the supermarket.
He	*did not*	[need	TO] STUDY	for the test.
We	*do not*	[want	TO] DRIVE	the new car.

*NOTE: The root form of the verb is used with the negative.

Special Infinitive Verb: USED TO [always in the past tense]			
(S)	**(V)**	**Infinitive**	**Complement**
She	[used	TO] EAT	with her friends.
It	[used	TO] BE	easy to run fast.
You	[used	TO] WORK	at the Student Center.
They	[used	TO] COOK	pizza.
They	*did not* [used	TO] COOK	pizza.

Interviews with Students

Students at a U.S. university were asked, "What did you used to do before you came to the U.S. that you don't do now?" Here are some of their replies.

"I didn't USED TO wear jeans in my country. I USED TO buy many clothes in Taipei. Here at the university, almost everyone wears blue jeans, so now I wear jeans, too."

Hui-Ching Chang
Taiwan (R.O.C.)

"I USED TO go to the movies, but now I don't because the movies are in English, so I can't understand them."

Abdirizak Osman
Somalia

"I USED TO eat goat's meat, but now I HAVE TO eat beef because goat's meat is difficult to buy."

Salem Gaddah
Morocco

"I USED TO go to the office every day, and I USED TO have a salary every month. Now I am a student, so I NEED TO pay bills."

Kuo Mei Ping Yu
Taiwan (R.O.C.)

"In my country, I USED TO drive a car, but now I don't. I didn't USED TO ride a bicycle, but now I do. I WANT TO drive a car, but I can't."

Mohamed Al-Souhibani
Saudi Arabia

"I USED TO visit my family every weekend, and I USED TO drink coffee at six o'clock with my mother. Now my family is far away, so I HAVE TO drink coffee with my friends."

Mohamed Gaddah
Morocco

"I USED TO have many friends in my country. I don't know many people here. I WANT TO meet people, but it is difficult."

Fawzia Hajc Essr
Somalia

"I USED TO smoke a lot, but cigarettes are very expensive here. It's also bad for my health."

Takeshi Kanome
Japan

Don't kick against bricks.

translated by
Fugimoto Akira
Japan

Exercise 7B

With a small group of classmates, discuss what you USED TO do, what you NEED TO do, what you WANT TO do, and what you HAVE TO do. Take turns talking and using these specific infinitive verbs.

Writing Assignment

Describe a problem that you had and an adjustment that you made when you entered a new situation.

1. Use some of the questions that follow to help plan your paragraph.
   - What was the new situation?
   - Why were you involved in that situation?
   - What was puzzling? Strange? Unpleasant?
   - What was the problem?
   - Give an example of the problem.
   - How did you feel about the problem?
   - What adjustments did you make?
   - How did you solve the problem?
   - Did someone help you with the problem? How? In what ways?
   - Was your solution successful? How do you know?
   - What was the conclusion of the problem?

2. Exchange paragraphs with a classmate. Read the paragraph.
   A. Circle the infinitive verbs.
   B. Put parentheses ( ) around the adjectives.
   C. What questions could you ask your classmate about the paragraph?
   D. Underline any verb tense or spelling errors that you see in the paragraph. Discuss these errors with your classmate.

3. Revise your paragraph.
   A. Answer your classmate's questions about your paragraph.
   B. Make changes in your paragraph that will make it more interesting.

4. Rewrite your paragraph.

5. Share your paragraph with a small group of classmates.
   A. Read two to three paragraphs.
   B. Discuss why you liked one of the paragraphs with your small group.

Exercise 7C

With a partner, read the following paragraphs. Then do the exercises that follow each paragraph.

I

The Terrible Weather!

I am having trouble adjusting to the weather in Chicago. It is very cold. My friend, Carlos, _____ me that this winter has been one of the coldest since he _____ in Chicago. When I _____ to the university yesterday, my fingers and ears were freezing. I needed to buy winter clothing, so Carlos took me shopping after my class. I _____ to buy a hat, gloves, scarf, and moon boots. People call them moon boots because the astronauts wear them. Yesterday the temperature _____ minus eighteen degrees C., and today the temperature is minus seventeen degrees C. I also have to be careful of the snow and the ice wherever I walk. The weather here makes me walk fast because I want to go inside the heated buildings! I do not think I will adjust to this cold weather. Instead, I will wait for spring!

VERBS: arrive   be   have   tell   go

Maria Muñoz
Colombia

1. Write the correct past tense verbs in the blanks. Use each verb on the list only once.
2. Circle 3 special infinitive verbs: have to, want to, need to.
3. What is the main idea in the paragraph? Discuss your ideas with your partner.
4. There is one sentence that could be taken out of this paragraph because it is not about the main idea. Which sentence is that? Discuss your answer with your partner.

II

_____

About six years ago, my family and I _____ a cruise to the Bahamian Islands. I was so excited about the tour. But as we left the ship and walked through the town, I was shocked to see that most of the houses were small shacks made out of branches. The items that the owners of the houses were selling were all hand-crafted. The people _____ also much different than I expected. No one was dressed any better than I was, in my shorts and T-shirt. In fact, most of the people _____ hand-made shoes like thongs. As we ventured deeper into the village, people were sitting on the ground. A girl _____ my legs and said, "Sing a song for a quarter." One woman _____ to my sister, "Braid your hair for a quarter." Her English was broken, so she was hard to understand. I had never been in a society where people beg for things, and this was a big adjustment for me.

VERBS: be say wear take grab

Kelly Mehling
United States

1. Write the correct past tense verbs in the blanks. Use each verb on the list only once.

2. With your partner, write a title for this paragraph.

3. What is the main idea in the paragraph? Discuss your ideas with your partner.

4. What questions can you and your partner ask Kelly? How can he make his paragraph more interesting?

III

First Shopping Trip

My first shopping trip in the U.S. _____ a long time and troubled me
take
very much. It was the second morning after I arrived in the United States. After

breakfast, I _____ to the supermarket. When I _____ there, I
go **get**
_____ it was too early. The market was not open, so I had to wait for one hour.
find
When I _____ the market, I did not know what to do with my bag. I wanted
enter
to ask, but I _____ ashamed. I decided to observe for a while, and I
feel
_____ around the store, trying to find everything that I wanted. Finally, I
walk
_____ a salesman for assistance, and he _____ me that I needed to look
ask **tell**
at the signs hanging above. I was very glad to find a lot of things that I was looking

for. But another trouble was the English names of the goods. Many names

_____ very strange for me, so I _____ many things according to the
be **buy**

pictures on the package. I still made many mistakes. After I got home, I found many things were not what I wanted. I think the first time shopping was good practice for me. I _____ a lot, and now I am able to shop with confidence.
　　　　　learn

Shaoke Wang
China (P.R.C.)

1. Write the correct past tense verbs in the blanks.
2. (Circle) the special infinitive verbs: have to, need to, want to.
3. What problems did Wang have? How did he solve his problems?
4. Have you had a similar experience? Discuss your ideas with your partner.

> Reading thousands of books is good,
> but travelling thousands of miles is better.
>
> translated by
> *Hsiang-Rwei Tseng*
> Taiwan (R.O.C.)

Interview

Ask a friend NOT in your class to describe several problems and solutions he or she had in a new situation. Discuss the problems, and choose one problem. Ask your friend to describe that problem more completely.

1. Use some of the questions from the *Writing Assignment* on page 179 to complete the interview.

2. Write the paragraph about one of your friend's problems and one solution.

   A. Use past tense verbs and correct subject and object pronouns.

   B. Use connectors and adjectives.

   C. In some sentences use [, and] , [, but] or [, so] to join two clauses.

3. Exchange paragraphs with a classmate. Read the paragraph.

   A. What questions can you ask your classmate about the paragraph?

B. <u>Underline</u> any language errors you see in the paragraph.

C. Discuss the errors with your classmate, and help your classmate correct the errors.

4. Reread your paragraph.

A. What changes can you make to improve the paragraph?

B. What language errors should you correct?

5. Rewrite your paragraph.

JOINING CLAUSES WITH <u>BECAUSE</u>

Subject + Verb (+ Complement)

<u>BECAUSE</u>

Subject + Verb (+ Complement)

I was shocked BECAUSE people in the United States judge each other

strangely. U.S. professors grade students on class participation, class discussion,
            (S)   **(V)**   **(C)**   **(S)** **(V)**
and class presentations, so I am judged incompetent BECAUSE I believe that
         (S)(V)   **(C)**   **(S)** **(V)**
"silence is golden." It is painful for me to speak in class BECAUSE I grew up
      (C)
with Oriental sayings such as, "The one who talks most must be the least learned,"
                         (S) **(V)**   **(C)**
and "A big mouth is a big disaster." However, now I force myself to speak
          (S)   **(V)**   **(C)**
BECAUSE class participation helps my grade.

Gwin Li
China (P.R.C.)

Exercise 7D

With a partner, read the following personal letters. Then do the exercises that follow.

I

September 3, 1995

Dear Brother,

How are you? I am happy because my health is good, but I am sad because I am homesick. I hope all my brothers and sisters still remember me.

My English classes begin next week. However, I don't have enough money because I have to pay my rent. I need to have money to buy books, paper, and pens. I also want to buy the necessary study materials. Please tell our father about that.

I do not feel like a foreigner because the people are very nice. I am happy because I received a letter from you. Please write again.

Your brother,

Ameen Alawi

(United Arab Emirates)

1. Circle the BECAUSE that joins two clauses.
2. Underline the special infinitives: have to, need to, want to.
3. Make the underlined sentences negative.
4. What are the reasons that Ameen is happy?

II

November 14, 1995

Dear Mother,

How are you? I am fine. * I miss you. My dormitory is named Allison Hall. * My roommate is a pretty girl whose name is Jill. The university is very big. * I have to walk a lot. At first I was very tired because I had to walk so much, but now I like it.

There are people here from many parts of the world. I also have a Mexican friend. His name is Gerardo. * He is from Texas. Please write me. Mom, could you send me some Mexican candy (*pulpas, chilitos,* and *ticos*)?

Thanks with love,

Pilar Ortiz

(Mexico)

1. (Circle) the BECAUSE that joins two clauses.

2. Join two clauses with ⌐, and⌐ , ⌐, but⌐ or ⌐, so⌐ where you see the asterisks.

3. What questions could Pilar's mother ask her? Discuss your answers with your partner.

4. What other information could Pilar include in her letter? Discuss your answers with your partner.

III

February 10, 1996

Dear Father,

I'm writing this letter for my writing course, so I am going to tell you about my English classes. I began my program last month. At that time, I took a language placement examination, and my teachers decided that I needed to take four courses because my language proficiency was low. These courses are: Writing, Grammar, Reading, and Oral Communication. My teachers in all of these classes are very intelligent and understanding, and the courses are useful and interesting. Oral Communication is difficult because in this course I have to talk to Americans, and sometimes I meet unsociable people.

Besides my four classes each day, I also have other scheduled classes. Here is a copy of my weekly class schedule:

	M	T	W	TH	F
8–8:50	Writing	Writing	Writing	Writing	Writing
9–9:50	Reading	Reading	Reading	Reading	Reading
10–10:50					
11–11:50	Grammar	Grammar	Grammar	Grammar	Grammar
12–1	LUNCH!	LUNCH!	LUNCH!	LUNCH!	LUNCH!
1–1:50	Language Laboratory	Language Laboratory	Language Laboratory	Language Laboratory	Language Laboratory
2–2:50	Oral Communication	Oral Communication	Oral Communication	Oral Communication	Oral Communication
3–3:50	Pronunciation		Pronunciation		Pronunciation
4–4:50		Typing	Culture	Typing	

As you can see, Father, I am very busy. I study all day, and I need to do at least two hours of homework each night. I used to have time for pleasures and for hobbies, but now I don't have any free time. However, I am learning many things about English because I want to succeed in my university work.

Your son,

Saud Al-Battal

Saud Al-Battal

Saudi Arabia

1. (Circle) the BECAUSE that joins two clauses.

2. Underline 3 special infinitive verbs: have to, need to, and used to.

3. Why is Saud so busy?

4. Have you had a similar experience? Discuss your ideas with your partner.

Writing Assignment

With a partner, look at Saud's daily class schedule (in letter III). With your partner, write ONE paragraph that describes Saud's schedule. Use present tense verbs and time connectors (first, next, then, after that, finally). Answer some of the questions that follow:

- What time do Saud's classes begin?

- What time does Saud have to get up (probably)?

- What does Saud have to do every weekday (Monday through Friday)?

- What classes does Saud have every day?

- What other classes does Saud have?

- When does he have those classes?

- When does Saud arrive home from classes (probably)?

- What does Saud do in the evening (probably)?

- What time does Saud go to bed (probably)?

- With your partner, rewrite the paragraph. Change the verbs to past tense.

Many things look too difficult to complete, but if you persevere, you will be successful.

translated by
Hui Ching Chiang
Taiwan (R.O.C.)

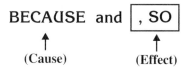

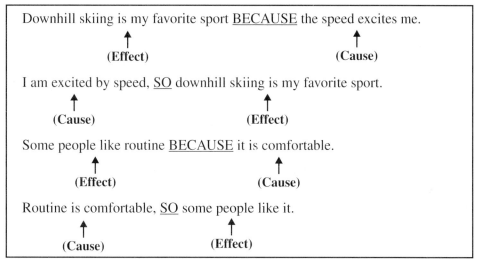

A Fable

Once upon a time there lived animals without any tails, and they all envied the fox <u>BECAUSE</u> he had a long bushy tail. One day the fox had the audacity to suggest that they all go to one African river <u>BECAUSE</u> the magic of the water would give them beautiful long tails. Of course, the fox had the advantage of his craftiness, and the other animals were weak in cunning, <u>SO</u> the animals agreed to travel to the magical African river. The fox suggested that he would first travel to the magical river to explore the place <u>BECAUSE</u> he wanted it to be safe for all the animals. The animals thought that the fox was very brave to sacrifice his safety for their sake, <u>SO</u> they encouraged him to take the trip. When the fox returned, pretending to be utterly exhausted, he told many dangerous stories about his adventures. He said that he had been tortured, and that the river was far too dangerous, <u>SO</u> he advised the animals not to go there. But the other animals continued to envy his beautiful tail, <u>SO</u> they ran to the river. Then they found that it was no use searching <u>BECAUSE</u> the fox's tail had been designed only for him. They were white with rage, but the sly little fox only laughed at them behind their backs.

Igor Ivanov
Barnaul, Siberia

Exercise 7E

With a small group of classmates, read the following paragraphs. Then do the exercises that follow each paragraph.

I

American Food

Although I could have chosen to cook Korean foods myself, I wanted to stay in a commercial dormitory during the first semester because I wanted to eat the food in the dormitory cafeteria. However, I had a very difficult time with American foods because I was not familiar with them, and their ingredients and cooking methods were different from those in Korea. Before I came to the U.S., I used to eat vegetable-based foods along with delicious Korean sauces. However, foods in the United States are mainly from animals, and sauces and dressings are different from those in Korea. For example, a typical meal in Korea consists of steamed sticky rice, a vegetable soup (Korean style), canned cabbage (*kimchi*), small dishes of fish or meat, and fresh vegetables with Korean sauces. A typical cafeteria meal in the United States consists of bread and potatoes, soup (American style), meat or fish, salads with dressings, and desserts. I had not eaten cereals for breakfast, or breads, or milk products (other than ice cream), so these foods did not seem appetizing to me. What I could eat without hesitation were fried eggs, steak, and ice cream, although even the steaks did not taste good to me. Another embarrassing thing was that at first I did not know the names of most main dishes, and I could not imagine the taste of the foods. Therefore, I chose foods by pointing to them instead of calling them by name. Then I had to memorize the shape and/ or color of foods and their taste, and to decide whether I could eat those again later or not. Fortunately, after the first month, the most difficult time passed, so I was able to choose foods I liked in the dormitory cafeteria.

Ray Cho
Korea

1. Underline 3 special infinitive verbs: have to, used to, want to.

2. Put parentheses ( ) around at least 6 adjectives in the paragraph.

3. Circle each BECAUSE and SO that join two clauses in the paragraph. Identify which part of each of those sentences are causes, and which are effects.

4. What are the similarities Ray discusses in this paragraph? What are the differences? Discuss your answers with your small group of classmates.

II

How Much? How Many?

"How many is it?"
"How many? As many as you want to buy!"
"But, no. I mean, which is the cost?"
"I don't know. I'm just selling them."
"I mean, how many dollars do I have to give you for it?"
"Oh,! You mean, 'How much is it?' O.K.! It is three dollars each."
"Oh—O.K."

For me, each conversation like this one, especially with someone from the U.S., represents a headache. I know grammar and vocabulary, and I put the words together as I learned in my English classes. But sometimes I forget a word and…then I have troubles. Nobody understands me, so I have to be thinking each moment about what I am saying. However, it is easier if I am talking to people who are also foreign in this country and are not English speakers. They are living my same experiences, so they understand the effort I am making with each phrase that I build up. If I make a mistake, they try to see what happened. Perhaps I am pronouncing a word in the wrong way, but communication can still go on. That is not the case when I am talking to U.S. citizens. They think they are wasting too much time in a conversation, or they think that I am stupid because I do not even know how to speak. I think this problem arises because U.S. citizens do not travel a lot outside their own country, so they are not in touch with other languages and cultures. I am sure that once a person goes to another country and has to talk in a foreign language, he or she will understand foreigners better. Then he or she will have the patience and the willingness to communicate with other people.

Maria Isabel DiMare
Costa Rica

1. Underline the present continuous verbs in the paragraph.

2. Circle each **BECAUSE** or SO that joins two clauses. Label what part of each of the sentences is the cause, and which is the effect.

3. Have you had an experience similar to Maria's? Discuss your ideas with your small group of classmates.

4. Use the chart below. With your classmates, decide how to explain to Maria how to correctly use "How much?" and "How many?"

HOW MUCH? and HOW MANY?

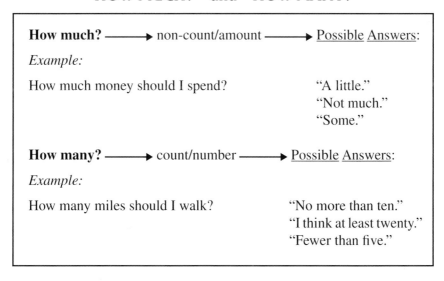

How much? ⟶ non-count/amount ⟶ Possible Answers:

Example:

How much money should I spend?   "A little."
"Not much."
"Some."

How many? ⟶ count/number ⟶ Possible Answers:

Example:

How many miles should I walk?   "No more than ten."
"I think at least twenty."
"Fewer than five."

III

Competition

The process of adjusting to American culture during my first months in the United States was very distressing because I was raised in a society where the sharing of lives is vital. American people live their own lives. * They do not share spontaneously with other people. I had imagined them as more friendly people. * I found myself in the middle of a cold atmosphere. One example of the attitude in the United States _____ the competition among university classmates. In graduate classes, the final grades people receive are usually based on the percentage of the rest of the group. This grading system _____ to complete isolationism among individuals because nobody can know, before an exam, what kind and what volume of information his classmates have. Having more information for an exam than the other people in the class makes one get a higher grade. Therefore, no one _____ his information or _____ with his classmates. These things made me feel unhappy until the day a classmate said "Hi!" and smiled at me. I realized then that the competition in the classroom does not need to interfere with friendship. * I have been much happier.

   VERBS: be   lead   share   study

Jorge Lopez Rendon
Colombia

1. Write the correct present tense verbs in the blanks. Use each verb on the list only once.

2. Join 2 clauses with ⬚ , and ⬚ or ⬚ , but ⬚ where you see the asterisks (*).

3. Put parentheses ( ) around at least 2 adjectives and 2 adverbs.

4. ⬭Circle⬮ each <u>BECAUSE</u> or <u>SO</u> that joins two clauses. Label what part of each of the sentences is the <u>cause</u>, and which is the <u>effect</u>. Discuss your answers with your small group of classmates.

> The depth of the sea can be predicted, but the depth of the heart: who knows?
>
> translated by
> *Ju Lun Lo*
> Indonesia

Writing Assignment

Write a paragraph about how your life changed because of a new situation or a new place. Use the chart that follows to plan your paragraph.

How My Life Has Changed

EFFECT:

the change in my life _____

_____

CAUSE(S):

why the change occurred _____

_____

the change in my life was good because _____

_____

_____

the change in my life was not good because _____

_____

_____

RESULTS:

the result(s) of the change in my life _____

_____

_____

---

1. Discuss your paragraph plan with a small group of classmates.

   A. What questions do your classmates have for you?

   B. What suggestions do your classmates have for you?

2. Discuss your classmates' paragraph plans.

   A. What questions do you have for your classmates?

   B. What suggestions do you have for your classmates?

3. Write your paragraph.

   A. Answer your classmates' questions.

   B. Use some of your classmates' suggestions to make your paragraph more interesting.

4. Share your paragraph with the same small group of classmates.

   A. Read two to three of your classmates' paragraphs.

   B. (Circle) any language problems you find.

   C. Write one suggestion at the end of each paragraph to improve that paragraph.

5. Now, reread your paragraph.

   A. Consider your classmates' suggestions.

   B. Correct any language problems.

6. Rewrite your paragraph.

Exercise 7F

With a partner, read the following paragraphs. Then, with your partner, do the exercises that follow each paragraph.

I

Commercial Centers in the United States

The most surprising thing about Gainesville, Florida, in comparison with my hometown in Belgium, is the quantity of commercial centers. During my first week in the United States, I walked down College Avenue. I had an endless choice of business centers. * Each had a huge supermarket. I was not used to this luxury and abundance, so I was very confused. In my hometown, we do not even have a shopping center. The small country village has only small shops, so buying groceries is a big event. I have to go from the bakery to the butcher. and from the cheese shop to the vegetable shop. I talk with the shop owners. * I buy what I need. The entire trip takes most of a morning because I have to go to so many shops. In the United States, I go shopping. * It does not take longer than one hour. The supermarket has all the items I want to buy in one store. The supermarket even has drugs and hardware for sale. I must admit that for students or bachelors, the supermarket is very practical. * It is certainly not as enjoyable as the more personalized shopping in my hometown.

Andre Emsens
Belgium

1. Join 2 clauses with $\boxed{\text{, and}}$ or $\boxed{\text{, but}}$ where you see the asterisks (*).

2. Put parentheses ( ) around at least 2 adjectives and 2 adverbs.

3. (Circle) each <u>BECAUSE</u> or <u>SO</u> that joins two clauses. Label what part of each of the sentences is the <u>cause</u>, and which is the <u>effect</u>. Discuss your answers with your partner.

4. Have you had a similar experience? Discuss your ideas with your partner.

II

Cultural Change

Having consecutive classes during lunchtime was the most distressing change for me. I had visited the U.S. before, so the American way of life was familiar to me. However. when I _____ attending classes, I _____ that the continuous daily working schedule from 8 A.M. to 5 P.M. was something I _____ not accustomed to. In my university job in Venezuela. the work schedule is from 8 to 12 and from 2 to 6. Here in the United States, the regular lunchtime is from 12 to 1. * People in my country usually have lunch between 12 and 2. Unfortunately, my fall semester schedule _____ consecutive classes at noon and at 1 P.M. * That really distressed me terribly. I could not understand why people here needed to have class lectures at noon, much less two consecutive classes. Consequently. the students cannot have lunch at the regular time. In my culture, lunchtime is usually respected. In addition, I need to have meals at very regular times because I have strict medical instructions. Therefore, I had a very difficult time adjusting to the new schedule.

VERBS: be   include   realize   start

Lucas Alvarez-Martinez
Venezuela

1. Write the correct past tense verbs in the blanks. Use each listed verb only once.

2. Join clauses with ⌐, and⌐ or ⌐, but⌐ where you see the asterisks (*).

3. What is the main idea in this paragraph? Discuss your answer with your partner.

4. What advice can you and your partner give to Lucas to help him solve his problem?

III

Relationships

In the past few months, my feelings about the relationship between my professors and me have changed a lot. In my country, I always thought that all of my professors were perfect. I felt that they never made any mistakes, even when my good friend told me that he knew that my professor had made some mistakes.

I never asked questions when I did not understand the lecture because I was afraid that I would say something wrong. I was afraid I would make my professors dislike me, so I only talked to them a few times. In contrast, I feel very different now. I really feel much more comfortable when I talk to my professors. * I realize that sometimes I make mistakes, and sometimes my professors make mistakes. too. Now, when I talk to my professors, I feel like I am talking to my good friend. * It is much easier to learn from a friend. The relationship between my professors and me has changed. * I learn more from school than ever.

Mai Anh Tran
Vietnam

1. Join 2 clauses with | , and | or | , but | where you see the asterisks (*).

2. Put parentheses ( ) around at least 2 adjectives and 2 adverbs.

3. (Circle) each <u>BECAUSE</u> or <u>SO</u> that joins two clauses. Label what part of each of the sentences is the <u>cause</u>, and which is the <u>effect</u>. Discuss your answers with your partner.

4. Look at all the paragraphs in this chapter. Which one (or ones) did you like most? Discuss your answers with your partner. Then discuss your answers with another set of partners.

> No one feels the fire except the person who steps in it.
>
> translated by
> *Fawzi El-Nassir*
> Iraq

Writing Assignment

Study the chart that follows. It gives recent trends of computer sales in the United States, and it predicts future computer sales (see the asterisk). Write a paragraph that describes the chart.

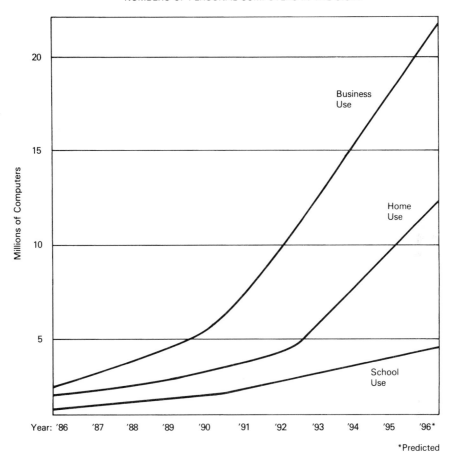

NUMBERS OF PERSONAL COMPUTERS IN THE U.S.A.

*Predicted

1. As you plan your paragraph,

    A. Use present and past tense verbs, and infinitive verbs.

    B. Use appropriate connectors.

    C. Use ⟨ , and ⟩ , ⟨ , but ⟩ or ⟨ , so ⟩ to join some clauses.

    D. Use some of the sentence structures that follow.

        • According to a survey by Creative Computing magazine,…

        • Before 1980, computer sales…

        • However, during the next few years,…

        • For example, computers sold to businesses…

        • In addition, computers sold for home use…

        • Schools also bought computers, but…

 • The survey predicts that… will be sold…

 • I think the reason(s) for the recent trends in U.S. computer sales is/are…

2. Exchange paragraphs with a partner. Read your partner's paragraph.

  A. Put a box around each ⌐, and⌐ and ⌐, but⌐ that joins two clauses.

  B. (Circle) each <u>BECAUSE</u> and <u>SO</u> that joins two clauses.

  C. <u>Underline</u> any language errors that you find.

3. With your partner, discuss differences between your paragraph and your partner's paragraph.

4. Reread your paragraph. Make changes that will improve your paragraph.

5. Rewrite your paragraph.

> Tell me who your friends are, and I'll tell you who you are.
>
> translated by
> *Khalid Al-Sadon*
> Saudi Arabia

Other Writing Topics

 • A Problem I Encountered Last Year

 • An Adjustment I Made in Childhood

 • A Dream I Had

 • My Favorite Activities in My Country

 • My Favorite Activities in the United States

 • A Person Who Changed My Life

Writing Projects

Individual Projects:

1. Write several paragraphs about changes that have happened to you because of a change in your life situation. Then submit the paragraphs to a student newspaper,

or make a booklet entitled "Adjustments." Illustrate the booklet with "before" and "after" drawings, charts, and photographs.

2. Individually, or with a partner, write several paragraphs about the registration process at your college or university. This booklet should help new students "survive" registration for courses. Information can include a map of the campus, a list of instructions, and the telephone numbers of important resource people. You might also answer some of the following questions:

-   What should a student do first? Second? Next? After that?
-   What problems will students encounter?
-   How can those problems be solved?
-   Who should students contact to help them solve their registration problems?
-   What offices on the campus are important for registering students? Why?

Group Project: Construct a housing survey like the one that follows. Ask international students NOT in your class to complete copies of the survey. Compile the surveys, and summarize the data in several paragraphs. Submit the results of the survey to the university Housing Office or the Foreign Student Office for incoming international students to use.

Sample Questionnaire

Country_____   M_____ F_____   Single_____ Married_____

Age_____   Graduate _____   Undergraduate _____

I LIVE IN

_____ an apartment   _____ a house   _____ a dorm room

I LIVE

_____ alone   _____ with a roommate (s)   _____ with my family

_____ with an American family   _____ other

How would you recommend your living situation to another international student?

_____ Excellent   _____ Good   _____ Bad

Sample Questionnaire (Continued)

Advantages of where you live:

	excellent	good	not too important
Low rent			
Food prepared			
Kept clean			
Close to campus			
Good roommate(s)			
Live alone			
Quiet			
Beautiful surroundings			

Disadvantages of where you live:

	terrible	bad	not too important
High rent			
Prepare my own food			
Clean it myself			
Far from campus			
Bad roommate(s)			
Live alone			
Noisy			
Ugly			

8

Similarities and Differences

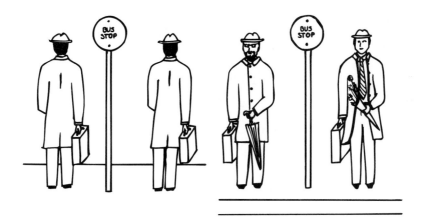

Breakfasts

Breakfast in my country is completely different from breakfast in the U.S. In Malaysia, for example, we eat the same foods for breakfast that we eat for lunch or for dinner: rice, meat, and vegetables. We do not specify what kind of food is suitable for breakfast. However, after I arrived in the U.S., I learned that Americans have very specific foods for breakfast: eggs, toast, pancakes, and juice. Another difference I discovered when I came to the United States was the attitude towards milk. In my country, if someone drinks milk in the morning, we say that he is poisoning his body. We think milk is very bad for our health. In the U.S., however, people drink milk every morning, and they believe that milk is "the most perfect food." I am very confused about these differences, but I am sure I will adjust to them.

Chia-Chon Pin
Malaysia

Light your own house before you light the others.

translated by
Jamal Jawad
Sierra Leone

TIME CLAUSES

Time Words: BEFORE   AFTER   WHEN

Structures = TIME WORD + S + V (+ C), S + V (+ C)

OR

S + V (+ C) **TIME WORD + S + V (+ C).**

Examples

[WHEN] I go to the supermarket, I buy many foods.

OR

I buy many foods [WHEN] I go to the supermarket.

[BEFORE] I came to the U.S., I never watched television.

OR

I never watched television [BEFORE] I came to the U.S.

[AFTER] I finish my university work, I will be an engineer.

OR

I will be an engineer [AFTER] I finish my university work.

Breakfast

BEFORE I left Japan, I did not think about American food. But WHEN I was on the jet, the flight attendant brought me a very strange breakfast. I had a cup of coffee, cookies, bread and butter, and some fruit. The meal was so simple that I was not completely satisfied. I wanted to have another meal soon. In Japan, we have rice, miso soup, tofu (soybean pudding), and some pickles for breakfast. We often put some seafood into the miso soup, such as octopus, seaplant, seafly, or seaworm. AFTER we finish breakfast in Japan, we feel satisfied because the meal is light, not greasy, and good for our health.

Misuaki Uchida
Japan

Exercise 8A

With a partner, connect each pair of clauses below with a time word (before, after, or when). Write each sentence twice, using both structures described above. Some of the sentences can be written with two or even all three of the time words, but the meaning of the sentence will change. Discuss these changes with your partner.

A. Natalia wrote me. She received my letter.

    1. _____

    2. _____

B. We went to the movies. We went to a pizza restaurant.

    1. _____

    2. _____

C. I like to write late at night. It is cool.

    1. _____

    2. _____

D. Lars wears old, cozy clothes. He writes his essays for school.

    1. _____

    2. _____

E. India achieved independence. Many women began to practice Classical Dance.

    1. _____

    2. _____

> Time always puts things in the right place.
>
> translated by
> *Fausto Ibarra*
> Mexico

Exercise 8B

With a partner or a small group of classmates, read the following paragraphs. Then do the exercises that follow each paragraph.

I

Breakfast Differences

There _____ several differences between breakfast in my country and breakfast in the U.S. First, before I came to the United States, I ate breakfast with my family every day. Now, I _____ alone, so I often _____ television when I eat my breakfast. Second, in my country, Venezuela, people usually _____ at 6 A.M. because they begin work at 7 A.M. However, in the U.S., people go to work at 9 A.M., so they usually eat breakfast later. Finally, people in my country always _____ breakfast because they think that it is the most important meal of the day. However, in the United States, people sometimes do not have breakfast. They drink coffee, but they do not eat anything.

VERBS: be   begin   eat   have   watch

Raquel Pedroza
Venezuela

1. Write the correct present tense verbs in the blanks. Use each verb on the list only once.
2. Underline the time clauses in the paragraph. (Circle) the time word in each clause: BEFORE, AFTER, WHEN.
3. Put parentheses ( ) around 4 adverbs of frequency.
4. Do you think that Raquel prefers breakfast in Venezuela or breakfast in the U.S.?
5. Discuss your answer with your partner or your group.

II

Breakfast in My Country and in the United States

In my country, breakfast is not the same as it is in the United States. When I _____ in my country, I _____ a small breakfast of hot milk, coffee, fresh bread, jelly, butter, and cheese. Every day I _____ almost the same foods. However, after I _____ in the United States, I _____ that breakfast is a much more important meal. I live with an American family, and every morning we have a large meal. We eat bacon and eggs, toast, butter and jelly, cottage cheese, coffee or tea, cold milk, and orange juice. Before I _____ to the United States, I never _____ that breakfast was a very interesting or important meal, but now I have changed my mind, and I enjoy eating breakfast.

VERBS: arrive be come eat find have think

Marlene Clerc
Switzerland

1. Write the correct past tense verbs in the blanks. Use each verb on the list only once.

2. <u>Underline</u> 3 time clauses in the paragraph. (Circle) the time word in each clause: WHEN, BEFORE, AFTER.

3. Put parentheses ( ) around at least 5 adjectives.

4. What are the differences between breakfast in Switzerland and breakfast in the United States? Discuss your answer with your partner or your group.

The frugal man eats his dinner twice.

translated by
Youssef El-Tayash
Libya

COMPARATIVE ADJECTIVES*

S + V	**+ short ADJECTIVE + -ER +**	(**THAN**	+ Complement)
Lorena is	TALLER	THAN	Faiza.
The small class was	QUIETER	THAN	the large class.
This test seemed	EASIER	THAN	that one.
He ran	FASTER	THAN	his brother, and
he is	STRONGER too.		

S + V + MORE (LESS) + long ADJECTIVE + (THAN + Complement)

Maria's book is	MORE INTERESTING	THAN	mine.
Learning English is	MORE DIFFICULT	THAN	learning Spanish.
U.S. supermarkets are	MORE CONVENIENT	THAN	grocery stores in my country, but
they are also	MORE EXPENSIVE.		

NOTE: See the spelling rules in Appendix C.

Two Food Stores

One difference between Boston and my hometown, Yaizu, is the size of the food stores. For example, Safeway, which is one of the grocery stores in Boston, has a huge parking lot in front of the building because many customers drive their cars to the store. A lot of carts are at the entrance of the supermarket, so it is easy for people to buy many groceries just once a month. Inside the supermarkets, the aisles occupy a large part of the room, so people can shop comfortably. In contrast, Yakumo Store, one of the grocery stores in Yaizu, is much SMALLER THAN Safeway, and it is also LESS COMFORTABLE. Yakumo Store does not have a parking lot because most customers come from neighboring houses. Also, customers use small, hand-carried baskets because they usually buy food for only one or two days. The size of the store is a quarter of Safeway. A lot of food is crammed into the refrigerators and the shelves, so the store is LESS CONVENIENT THAN Safeway. However, the customers take only ten or twenty minutes to buy food for that evening, so the convenience is not important. Finally, both Safeway and Yakumo Store serve their customers adequately, but I think Safeway has <u>MORE PLEASANT</u> surroundings.

Hidekazu Oishi
Japan

Exercise 8C

With a small group of classmates, read the following paragraphs. Then do the exercises that follow each paragraph.

I

Shopping in the U.S. and Paraguay

There are several differences between shopping for food in my country and shopping for food in the U.S. First, in Paraguay, there are many small stores around the city, so I do not have to travel to buy food. In the U.S., however, the supermarkets are fewer and larger, and they are not located in neighborhoods where people live. Therefore, I must drive my car to the supermarket. Second, the time for shopping in Paraguay and in the U.S. differs. In my country, people usually go to the food stores after they have finished their jobs, in the first hours of the night. In contrast, people in the U.S. are accustomed to shopping when they have more time. They usually go to the supermarkets on the weekends, especially on Saturday morning, and they even shop on Sundays. Finally, people in Paraguay and the U.S. shop for different amounts of food. In my country, the selection of foods is smaller and the foods are much fresher than foods in the U.S. supermarkets. Moreover many people in Paraguay are not able to preserve their food because they do not have refrigerators, so they buy only enough food for the day. In contrast, people in the United States often buy canned and frozen foods that they can keep for several weeks or months, so their shopping trips are more efficient and more complete.

Cesar Prieto
Paraguay

1. <u>Underline</u> 4 short comparative adjectives and 2 long comparative adjectives in the paragraph.

2. Put 2 time clauses in parentheses ( ), and (circle) the "time" word in each clause.

3. (Circle) <u>BECAUSE</u> and <u>SO</u> when they join two clauses. Identify which part of each sentence is the cause and which is the effect. Discuss your answer with your group.

4. What are the differences between shopping in Paraguay and shopping in the U.S? Discuss your answers with your group.

II
Differences in Shopping

My country, Sudan, is poorer than the U.S. * There are differences between shopping for food there and shopping for food in the U.S. When I came to the U.S., the supermarkets surprised me because they sell everything. In my country, I have to go to many stores to collect the foods I need because the stores belong to individual persons, and they do not have much money to buy many foods. But the U.S. supermarket is much more convenient. I can buy meat, bread, vegetables, drugs, auto supplies, and even clothing at just one large store. I was also surprised at the hours for shopping in the U.S. The supermarkets are almost always open. * In my country, I have to shop during specific hours because the food comes from the rural areas. There are no refrigerators for storage. * The food is limited. For example, if I want to buy fresh vegetables, I need to go to the store early. Finally, the supermarkets in the U.S. have a much larger selection of foods. * I can always find what I want to buy. In my country, I have fewer choices. For all these reasons, I think that U.S. supermarkets are richer and more developed than food stores in Sudan.

Tariq Ahmed Habbas
Sudan

1. <u>Underline</u> 4 short comparative adjectives and 2 long comparative adjectives in the paragraph.

2. Join 2 clauses with ⎡ , but, ⎤ , ⎡ , so ⎤ or ⎡ because ⎤ wherever you see an asterisk (*).

3. Put parentheses ( ) around the special verbs: *have to, want to, need to*.

4. In what ways is Tariq's paragraph similar to Cesar's and Hidekazu's paragraphs? In what ways is it different? Discuss your answers with your group.

> The faster you run, the faster you die.
>
>
>
> translated by
> *Claude Combo*
> Burkina Faso
>
>

Writing Assignment

Choose two stores, or two *kinds* of stores, that you have in your country. Write a paragraph for a classmate who is NOT from your country that describes the similarities and the differences between the two stores.

Examples

2 food stores	*OR*	1 department store and 1 gift shop
2 clothing stores	*OR*	1 fruit store and 1 bakery
2 open air markets	*OR*	_____

1. Use the chart that follows to plan your paragraph.

TWO STORES

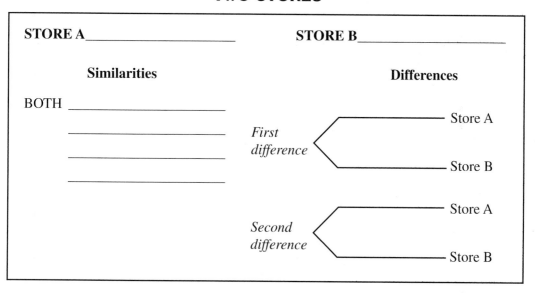

2. As you plan and write your paragraph,

    A. Use short and long comparative adjectives.

    B. Use some time clauses.

    C. Use some of the following comparison structures.

COMPARISON STRUCTURES

X	is	AS tall	AS	Y.
X	is	SIMILAR	TO	Y.
X	is	THE SAME	AS	Y.
BOTH X		and Y are…		
LIKE X,		Y is…		
There are SIMILARITIES BETWEEN			X and Y.	

D. Use some of the following contrast structures:

CONTRAST STRUCTURES

X	is	DIFFERENT FROM	Y.
X	is	DIFFERENT THAN	Y.
X		DIFFERS FROM	Y.

3. Exchange paragraphs with a classmate. Read your partner's paragraph.

A. (Circle) the short and long comparative adjectives.

B. Put parentheses ( ) around the time clauses.

C. Put brackets [ ] around the time words in the paragraph.

D. Underline any language errors you see in the paragraph. Discuss these errors with your partner, and help your partner correct the errors.

E. Tell your partner what you most like about her/his paragraph.

F. Make one to three suggestions about how to improve the paragraph.

4. Reread your paragraph. Make the changes that will make your paragraph more successful.

5. Rewrite your paragraph. Share your paragraph with a small group of classmates.

6. Discuss with your group the paragraph you liked best.

Exercise 8D

With a small group of classmates, read the following paragraphs. Then do the exercises that follow each paragraph.

I

How My Life Has Changed

My life has changed twice during the last three years. In my country, high school graduates have to serve in the National Guard for 26 months. I had no choice, so I followed my fortune. I entered the army at the age of twenty-two. The first change I had to face was that as a soldier, I had to obey orders with a smile. * I had to carry out the missions assigned by my superiors. Failure is not accepted in the army. In fact, it is punished. In addition, I had to awake at 5:30 A.M. because that was my official schedule. I had to get washed, shaved, and dressed in my green uniform within fifteen minutes. After breakfast, from 6:00 A.M. until 7 P.M., I worked very hard at my job. * I trained with guns. Even my bedtime was regulated by my superiors. In contrast, today no one tells me what to do! As a university student, I am completely responsible for my schedule. * I do not have to obey orders. Therefore, I never get up before 8 A.M. * I choose the time to have breakfast. Until lunch, I use my time to attend classes, to sport around, to go shopping, or to sleep. In the afternoon, I study, rest, or even work on a computer. At night, I can do anything I feel like: go to a movie, watch television, listen to music, or talk with my friends. I can finally wear the clothes I want: jeans, a three-piece suit, or shorts! In conclusion, even though I believe in the defense of my country, I prefer the life of a student!

Pavlos G. Alexandros
Cyprus

1. Join clauses with , and or , but where you see the asterisks (*).

2. Put parentheses ( ) around at least 2 adjectives and 2 adverbs.

3. Circle each <u>BECAUSE</u> or <u>SO</u> that joins two clauses. Label the part of each sentence that is the <u>cause</u> and the part that is the <u>effect</u>. Discuss your answers with your small group of classmates.

4. What is the main idea in this paragraph? Discuss your answer with your group.

II

China and Kyrgyzstan

Living in Bishkek is far easier than living in Harbin, China. First, I live in the suburbs, so I do not have to deal with as much pollution as I did in Harbin, a crowded city of three million people. In Harbin, the coal dust was quite thick; I knew I was inhaling pollution. * The pollution didn't allow me to see the scenery outside the city. Also, because I live in the suburbs, I have a large, spacious apartment rather than a small place to live. From my windows on the 7th floor, I can see a clear, beautiful view of the western sky at sunset. * There are mountains on both the east and the west that make my surroundings spectacular. Finally, I am not stared at for being a foreigner. In fact, I fit in so well that I am often asked what time it is or some other such questions, which, of course, I can't answer! Instead, I tell them, "No Russian, sorry." They smile, since they feel they have been pleasantly fooled. * I smile since I like the fact that they think I am Russian. But there is one way in which Bishkek and Harbin are the same: in both places I have chosen to avoid public transportation because the crowding is intense, so I walk everywhere I go—I do get a lot of exercise!

Kristina Gray
United States

1. Join clauses with $\boxed{\text{, and}}$ where you see the asterisks (*).

2. <u>Underline</u> the connectors in the paragraph.

3. (Circle) each <u>BECAUSE</u> or ,<u>SO</u> that joins two clauses. Label the part of each of the sentence that is the <u>cause</u>, and the part that is the <u>effect</u>. Discuss your answers with your small group of classmates.

4. What is the main idea in this paragraph? Discuss your answer with your group.

A secret between more than two is no secret.

translated by
Saad Shukar
Iraq

Interview

Ask a person NOT in your class and NOT from your country to describe a food store in his or her country. Make a chart like the one in the *Writing Assignment* on pages 206–207, and write the similarities and differences between that person's description and a food store in your country. Then write a paragraph that compares the two stores.

1. As you write your paragraph,

    A. Use comparative adjectives.

    B. Use some of the comparison and contrast sentence structures in the *Writing Assignment.*

2. With a small group of classmates, read two to three paragraphs. At the end of each paragraph,

    A. Write one suggestion to make the paragraph more interesting.

    B. Write one question that will help the author of the paragraph revise his or her paragraph.

3. Reread your paragraph. Use the suggestions and questions from your classmates to revise your paragraph. Make changes that will improve your paragraph.

4. Rewrite your paragraph.

COMPARISON AMONG THREE OR MORE

S	+	V	+ <u>**THE**</u> + short <u>**ADJECTIVE**</u> + <u>**-EST**</u> (+ Complement)

Mehdi	is	THE TALL**EST**	man in the class.

Morellais	is	THE HAPPI**EST**	
		THE PRETTI**EST**	and girl in her family.

The trip	was	THE LONG**EST**	we had taken.

They	carried	THE HEAVI**EST**	box upstairs.

S	+	V	+ <u>**THE**</u> + <u>**MOST (LEAST)**</u> + long <u>**ADJECTIVE**</u> + <u>**-EST**</u> (+ C)

We	were	THE MOST WORRIED passengers on the airplane.

Finding an apartment	was	THE MOST FRUSTRATING job I ever had.

Hassan	is	THE MOST SUCCESSFUL graduate student of all.

Her flower garden	is	THE MOST FRAGRANT on the street.

EXCEPTIONS

	Comparison between 2	Comparison among 3 or more
GOOD	BETTER THAN	THE BEST
BAD	WORSE THAN	THE WORST

Examples

Man-Chiu played soccer <u>BETTER THAN</u> Elmi.

Professor Berry was <u>THE BEST</u> teacher I have had.

The statistics exam was <u>WORSE THAN</u> the math exam.

That was <u>THE WORST</u> experience I ever faced.

Teachers

I have attended schools in three countries—Colombia, Mexico, and the United States—and my opinion is that North American teachers are <u>THE MOST FRIENDLY</u>, Mexican teachers are <u>THE STRICTEST</u>, and Colombian teachers are <u>THE LEAST SENSITIVE</u>. In their attitudes towards their jobs, teachers in these countries are very different. In Colombia, most of the teachers are people whose main purpose is far from teaching. These teachers look at their jobs as something worthless, and they look at their students as another piece of furniture in the classroom. In Mexico, the teachers are very strict. For example, even if you pass your exams, if your behavior is not good, you will not pass to the next level. The situation is different in the U.S. North American teachers look at their students as intelligent beings, and they worry about their students. There is not much distance between the teachers and their students, and some teachers let their students call them by their first names!

Graciano Cauldron
Colombia

> To meet someone by chance is sometimes better than a thousand appointments.
>
> translated by
> *Joharah Nihidh*
> Saudi Arabia

Exercise 8E

With a small group of classmates, read the following paragraphs. Identify the main idea of each paragraph. Use a chart like the one that follows to make a list of the similarities and the differences. Then do the exercises that follow each paragraph.

MAIN IDEA: _____

Similarities	**Differences**
_____	_____
_____	_____
_____	_____
_____	_____

I

Teachers

In my country, teachers are the most important workers for the community. They have the highest salaries and the shortest time of working. However, I have learned that teachers in the United States do not have as much income as teachers in Kuwait. * They work harder and longer hours. Another difference is that in Kuwait, we do not have any women teachers in men's schools. * In the United States, many teachers are women. I find this very strange and unusual. Finally, in my country, teachers have a stronger relationship with their students than teachers in the United States. I think that this is because of the shared language and because of the longer time that students study with their teachers. In Kuwait, teachers teach their students all day for a year. * In the United States, students meet with several teachers, one for each class. * Classes last a shorter time, sometimes only two months. For these reasons, I prefer the teachers in Kuwait.

Naser Al-Gabandi
Kuwait

1. <u>Underline</u> 5 comparative adjectives in the paragraph.

2. Put parentheses ( ) around the negative verbs.

3. Put brackets [ ] around 5 prepositional phrases. (Circle) the noun (or the pronoun) that follows each preposition.

4. Join 2 sentences with | , and | or | , but | where you see the asterisks (*).

II

Differences Between Teachers

I think that there are many differences between teachers in the United States and teachers in my country. First, U.S. teachers are more involved in their teaching than the teachers in Iraq. I think this is because teachers in my country must teach more than thirty students in a class, but in my U.S classes there are only ten to twelve students. Second, U.S. teachers are freer in their methods than Iraqi teachers. Iraqi teachers have fixed schedules and classical methods, but U.S. teachers use techniques like role playing and equipment like computers. Finally, the most important difference between U.S. teachers and Iraqi teachers is their evaluation procedures. In my country, students must pass only one examination, but in the United States, students have many assignments and quizzes, so their success depends on many different things.

Hatim Al-Kinani
Iraq

1. Put parentheses ( ) around 3 comparative adjectives.

2. (Circle) 3 connectors in the paragraph.

3. Could Hatim write more than one paragraph about her idea? Discuss your answer with your small group of classmates.

4. Compare and contrast Hatim's paragraph with Naser's paragraph (Paragraph I). In what ways are their ideas similar? In what ways are they different? Discuss your answers with your group.

> It is better to study nothing than to study a lot without thinking.
>
> translated by
> *John Shyh-Yuan Wang*
> China (P.R.C.)

Writing Assignment

Write a paragraph about the best teacher *OR* the best course you have had.

1. As you plan your paragraph,

   A. Answer some of the questions below.

   • Who was your best teacher? *OR* Which class was your best class?

   • What qualities made that teacher (or class) the best?

   B. Give examples to show why you chose that teacher or course.

   • Why did you especially like that teacher (or class)?

   because _____

   For example, _____

   _____

   because _____

   For example, _____

   _____

   because _____

   For example, _____

   _____

2. As you write your paragraph,

    A. Use comparative adjectives.

    B. Use BECAUSE or ,SO to join clauses.

    C. Use | , and | or | , but | to join clauses.

3. Share your paragraph with a partner. Read your partner's paragraph, and

    A. (Circle) comparative adjectives.

    B. Put brackets [ ] around <u>BECAUSE</u> and ,<u>SO</u> that join clauses.

    C. Put boxes around | , and | or | , but | that join clauses.

4. To help your partner,

    A. Ask questions that will make the paragraph more interesting.

    B. Give suggestions that will make the paragraph more interesting.

    C. <u>Underline</u> any language problems that you find.

5. Now, reread your paragraph. Use your partner's questions and suggestions to revise your paragraph.

6. Rewrite your paragraph.

> The monk from far away
> knows much more about the Bible
> than the monk who lives here.
>
> translated by
> *Hsiang-Rwei Tseng*
> Taiwan (R.O.C.)

Exercise 8F

Read the following paragraphs. Join two clauses with | , and | , | , but | , | , so | *or* | because | *wherever you see an asterisk (*).*

I

Television

There are two great differences between television in my country, which is Tunisia, and television in the U.S. For example, in Tunisia, we have fewer channels (only two). The first is in Arabic. * The second is in French. In the U.S., however, there are so many channels that I cannot count them. * All of them are in English. Of course, in Tunisia, we can watch a lot of channels from Italy. * The programs are in Italian. * When we watch, we do not understand anything. Before I came to the U.S., I used to watch soccer matches in Italian because I did not need to listen to the language. I also watched some films in Italian. * I had already seen them in French. The other most essential difference between television in Tunisia and television in the U.S. is the ownership of the television stations. Tunisian television is controlled by the government. * There are many political programs that deal with the party that is governing the country. In contrast, U.S. television is privately owned. The stations broadcast many, many advertisements to earn money. * They are less interested in politics. I do not like the interruptions of these advertisements. * I prefer television in my country.

Sofouen Ben Brahim
Tunisia

II
Similarities in Television Programs

In Mexico City, many television programs are the same as those in the U.S., but there are some differences. For example, many of the television series are the same. * They are spoken in Spanish instead of English. We have dramas and news, sports and movies on Mexican television. Of course, some programs are different. For example, on game shows in both countries, the purpose is for the contestants to win money. * On the U.S. game shows, you need more luck, while on Mexican game shows, you need more agility. Finally, Mexico City has cablevision just like the U.S. * We have many channels. Some are in English. * Many children learn English by watching T.V. Some of the channels have special programs just for children. * On other channels, there are just movies or just sports. In short, television in my country is similar to television in the U.S.

Elias Rodriquez
Mexico

The flower blooms in inspiration and follows the mind.
If people feel lonely, flower lives with people.
If people feel sorrow, flower walks with people.

translated by
Chul Ha Lee
Korea

Collaborative Writing Assignment

With a partner, study the chart below. Then, with your partner, write <u>one</u> paragraph about prices for food in Atlanta and prices for food in your hometown.

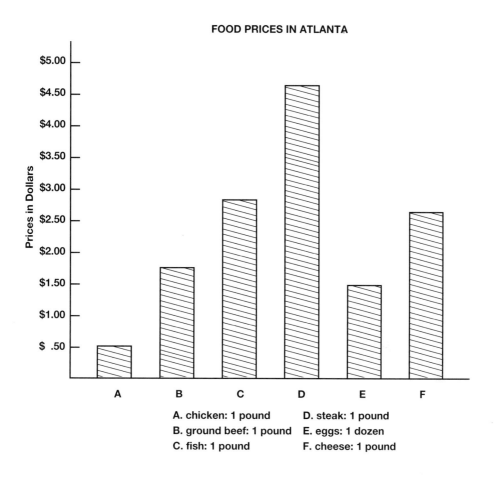

FOOD PRICES IN ATLANTA

A. chicken: 1 pound   D. steak: 1 pound
B. ground beef: 1 pound   E. eggs: 1 dozen
C. fish: 1 pound   F. cheese: 1 pound

1. As you plan your paragraph, answer the following questions:

   • What foods are cheaper than fish in Atlanta?
   • What is the most expensive food on the chart?
   • What is the cheapest food on the chart?
   • What foods are more expensive than cheese?
   • Are the foods in Atlanta more expensive than the same foods in your hometown?
   • What foods in Atlanta are too expensive to buy?
   • What foods are good bargains?
   • Would you buy chicken in Atlanta? Beef? Eggs? Why? Why not?

- Where do you shop for food in your hometown?
- What does the store look like?
- Where is it located?
- What foods are available in the store?
- What foods are good bargains?
- Would you buy chicken in the store in your hometown? Beef? Eggs? Why? Why not?

2. As you write the paragraph,

   A. Use comparative adjectives.

   B. Use <u>BECAUSE</u> and ,<u>SO</u> to join clauses.

   C. Use ⌐ , and ⌐ or ⌐ , but ⌐ to join clauses.

3. Share your paragraph with another set of partners.

Exercise 8G

With a small group of classmates, read the following paragraphs about various aspects of U.S. life that students found different from their home countries. Then do the exercises that follow each paragraph.

I

Transportation

Although my hometown, Ipoh, and Pocatello both have bus transportation, the use of mass transportation in the two cities is very different. Middle-income residents in Ipoh use the buses more often than people in Pocatello because the buses in Ipoh are more numerous and operate more efficiently. For example, buses in Ipoh do not stop at every busy stop. They stop when there are customers who want to board the buses. Furthermore, residents in Ipoh only have to wait ten minutes at the most before the bus arrives, so they will usually get to work on time. In addition, the price of the bus fare is only twenty cents (in American currency). On the other hand, buses in Pocatello stop at every bus stop, even when no one wants to leave or board the bus. Moreover, residents have to wait at least thirty minutes before they catch the next bus. As a result, many people arrive late to their appointments and are more frustrated than people in Ipoh. Finally, the bus fare in Pocatello is much more expensive: fifty cents. For these reasons, I prefer the buses in Ipoh to the buses in Pocatello.

Chee Siou
Malaysia

1. Put brackets [ ] around the comparison and contrast structures in the first sentence of this paragraph.

2. <u>Underline</u> 4 time clauses. Identify the subject (S) and the verb (V) in each time clause.

3. Put parentheses ( ) around 5 comparative adjectives in the paragraphs.

4. (Circle) 6 connectors in the paragraph. Identify each connector as a connector of <u>additional information</u> *OR* <u>contrasting information</u> *OR* <u>cause-effect information</u>.

II

Americans and Their Pets

After I had lived in Taiwan for twenty years, I was quite surprised to see that the American people are much more affectionate toward their pets than people in my country. Two years ago, when I first arrived in the United States, I took a walk to the small park near my house. I saw several people playing games with their pets, and if their pets did a good job, their masters would reward them with food or even with kisses. There were also people carefully combing their dogs' hair or clipping their dogs' nails. I had never seen that in my life! Therefore, I was totally dumbfounded. Later, when I was at the supermarket, I saw a multitude of frivolous and crazy pet foods and cosmetics: dog shampoo, kitty candy, pet clippers, and jeweled cat collars. I was shocked by how much care people showed toward their pets. Compared to the treatment pets get in my country, animals in America live a life of luxury. In Taiwan, people are much less concerned about their pets. People usually feed pets with their leftovers, and they do not give their pets special treats. In fact, people in Taiwan do not allow their pets to enter their houses. No matter how bad the weather is, the pets always have to stay outside. Finally, people in my country would never kiss their animals!

Hsiu-Yueh Chiu
Taiwan (R.O.C.)

1. <u>Underline</u> 2 comparative adjectives in the paragraph.

2. Put parentheses ( ) around 3 time clauses. (Circle) the time word for each clause.

3. Put brackets [ ] around 4 adverbs of frequency.

4. Have you had a similar experience? Discuss your answer with your small group of classmates.

III

Traffic Rules

When I first came to Ashland, I noticed how different the traffic in the downtown area was from my home city, Bangladore. Even though there are many traffic rules in Bangladore, not one person follows them. But here, in Ohio, most people follow the traffic regulations. For example, they stop at every stop sign, even the middle of the night when there is no traffic at all. Back home the streets are much narrower compared to the broad roads in Ashland. Moreover, in downtown Bangladore, lots of people walk in the streets instead of the footpaths (sidewalks) because the footpaths are often used as parking spaces for scooters and motorcycles (and at times, cars as well!). However, in downtown Ashland, the sidewalks are used for people to walk, and parking spaces for vehicles are provided in the center of the streets. Another difference between these two cities is that there are no buses allowed in the downtown area of Bangladore, but quite a few buses go through the wide streets in Ashland. Finally, the overall scene in Bangladore is one of noise and crowds: lots of bullock carts transporting goods, car horns honking all the time, and many, many people. But here in Ashland, it is very quiet and peaceful in the downtown area, and horns are used only to greet friends.

Kamala Vedanthan
Bangladesh

1. Underline at least 5 prepositional phrases in the paragraph.

2. Put parentheses ( ) around at least 5 connectors in the paragraph. Identify each connector as an additional information *OR* a contrasting information *OR* a cause-effect information connector.

3. What is the main idea in this paragraph? Could Kamala write more than one paragraph about this topic? Discuss your answers with your group.

4. Have you had a similar experience? Discuss your answer with your group.

A tick far across the ocean can clearly be seen,
but an elephant in front of the eyes can't be seen.

translated by
Ju Lun Lo
Indonesia

Interview

Ask a person NOT in your class to describe several similarities and differences between his or her country and another country. Discuss what similarity or difference would be most interesting to write about. Ask some of the questions that follow, and use the chart to help plan your paragraph.

- What are some similarities you noticed?

- What are some differences?

- What ONE similarity or difference was the most memorable?

- What made it memorable? Give an example.

- Why do you remember it? Give another example.

SIMILARITIES AND DIFFERENCES

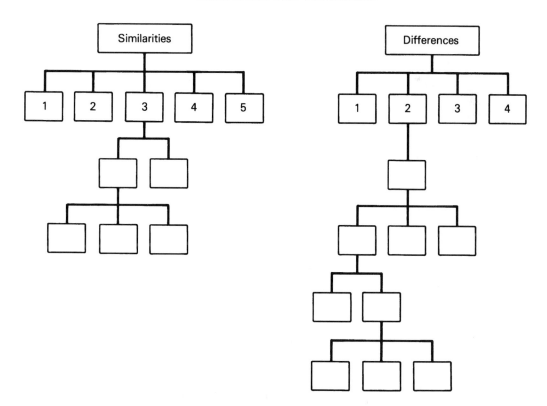

1. As you plan your paragraph

    A. Use comparison and/or contrast structures.

    B. Use past tense, and use connectors.

2. Write the paragraph. After you finish, reread your paragraph.

    A. Is there anything you want to add?

    B. Are there any language problems that you need to correct?

3. Exchange paragraphs with a classmate. Read the paragraph.

    A. Put parentheses ( ) around any comparison or contrast structures.

    B. (Circle) the connectors in the paragraph.

    C. Underline any language errors you find in the paragraph. Discuss those errors with your classmate, and help correct the errors.

    D. Ask your classmate questions that will help improve her/his paragraph.

4. Using the help from your classmate, revise your paragraph. How can you make the paragraph more interesting?

5. Rewrite your paragraph.

6. Share your paragraph with a small group of classmates.

    A. Read two to three paragraphs.

    B. Discuss the paragraph your liked best with your classmates. Why did you like it best?

Exercise 8H

With a partner or a small group of classmates, read the following paragraphs. Then do the exercises that follow each paragraph.

I

Weekends

Weekends are more important for me in Egypt than weekends in the United States. In Egypt, I usually go to my father's ranch, which is about fifty miles from where I live in Cairo. There I usually do physical work, which I miss in my work in the university. I also go swimming in the lake close to our ranch. In the evening, I go back to Cairo where I meet all my brothers and sisters. We eat dinner with our parents in my older brother's home. After dinner we stay until late to discuss our personal problems and also to discuss the solutions. The evening is a good time for our children to play together and to become close to each other. That is important for all Egyptian families. <u>In contrast, my weekends in the United States are more lonely and more boring than they were in Egypt</u>. I usually study for my classes, go to the supermarket, and spend some of the day with my Egyptian friends in the Muslim meeting hall. When I have time, I drive to Seattle, and I sometimes telephone my brother in Houston. My weekends in Egypt were certainly better than my weekends in the United States, but I hope that after enough time my weekends here will be as beautiful as my weekends in my country.

Khadr Hassan
Egypt

1. Put parentheses ( ) around 4 comparative adjectives.

2. Put brackets [ ] around 2 time clauses. (Circle) the time word for each clause.

3. <u>Underline</u> the comparison structure in the last sentence.

4. Have you had a similar experience? Discuss your answer with your partner or your group.

II
Weekends in Tunisia and the United States

Like American students, Tunisians practice various activities on the weekends to enjoy themselves, but these activities _____ different from one country to the other because the two cultures are different. In fact, American students can make dates with their girlfriends to spend the weekend together. However, it is not polite in Tunisia to go with a girlfriend without marriage. In many other ways, however, students in both countries spend weekends in almost the same way. For example, both Tunisian and U.S. students can go on picnics, on trips to the mountains, or to other scenic places. Some _____ to go to the movies or to play electronic games. Other students spend their weekends in various clubs such as musical or dramatic clubs. Still others _____ the habit of going to a stadium every Sunday to watch matches or to play games like soccer and hockey. There are other students in both Tunisia and the United States who _____ their weekends studying and preparing their assignments. Finally, many students _____ home every weekend to see their friends and relatives.

VERBS: be   drive   have   prefer   spend

Zaher Rebai
Tunisia

1. Write the correct present tense verbs in the blanks. Use each verb on the list only once.

2. <u>Underline</u> 5 comparison or contrast structures in the paragraph.

3. (Circle) 5 infinitive verbs.

4. Put parentheses ( ) around the connectors in the paragraph. Identify them as <u>additional</u> information *OR* <u>contrasting</u> information *OR* <u>cause-effect information</u> connectors.

III

Weekends Here and There

<u>Weekends in my country, Kenya, are different than in the U.S.</u> <u>I have been in the U.S. for a month.</u> When Friday approaches, I think of how I will spend another boring weekend. I always have three activities on the weekend: washing my clothes, reading the newspapers, and doing my homework. Usually by Saturday afternoon I have finished these activities. The remaining one-and-a-half days I spend by reading other books, magazines, and newspapers, or by walking up and down in my room, or by watching TV. My room directly faces on the main street, so I keep on counting the number of cars passing on Plum Street. Oh! What a boring weekend! <u>Back home, Kenyan weekends are special days.</u> By Friday afternoon, one can tell by the smiles on the faces that the weekend is at the door: two good days of visiting friends, going to the movies, and travelling to the national parks. Many of us also think that the weekend is a good time to be with our animals, dipping, inoculating, and treating the sick animals, and counting the newborns and total number of the flock to learn whether any goats have been lost. Taking the animals to an open grassland, and watching them gripping grass between their jaws, makes me elated. Caring for the small lambs is another exciting adventure. When the lambs arrive at the green pastures, one can tell that Silas has had a good weekend by the way he stands, one leg across the other, the spear leaning against the shoulder, the sword hanging at his waist, and two sticks in his hands. <u>He whistles to communicate with his flock.</u>

Silas Parsitau
Kenya

1. Identify the subject (S) and the verb (V) in the <u>underlined</u> sentences.

2. Put parentheses ( ) around the contrast structure in the first sentence.

3. How do you think Silas felt as he wrote this paragraph? How do you know? Discuss your answers with your partner or your group.

4. Study the picture of Silas (as a young boy) on page 225. How do you feel about Silas? Discuss your answer with your partner or your group.

Writing Assignment

Find a photograph of yourself as a child. Compare the person in that photograph with the person you are now.

1. As you begin to plan your paragraph, answer some of the following questions:
   - Where were you when the photograph was taken?
   - How old were you?
   - What were you doing just before the photograph was taken?
   - How are you different now?
   - How are you the same?

2. As you write your paragraph,

    A. Use comparison and contrast structures.

    B. Use comparative adjectives.

    C. Use appropriate connectors.

3. Exchange paragraphs with a partner. As you read your partner's paragraph,

    A. Underline comparison and contrast structures.

    B. Circle comparative adjectives.

    C. Put brackets [ ] around connectors.

    D. Ask your partner questions, and make suggestions, so that your partner can improve his/her paragraph.

4. Reread your paragraph. What changes can you make to improve your paragraph?

5. Rewrite your paragraph.

6. Share your paragraph with a small group of classmates.

    A. Read two to three paragraphs.

    B. Which paragraph did you like best? Why? Discuss your answers with the small group of classmates.

> There is no ivory with a flaw.
>
> translated by
> *Hadi Pasaribu*

Collaborative Writing Assignment

With a partner, study the following chart. It shows the results of a survey of 807 U.S. television viewers. With your partner write one paragraph describing the chart.

SURVEY OF U.S. TELEVISION WATCHING HABITS

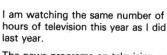

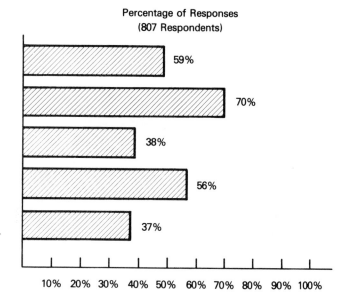

Survey Statements	Percentage of Responses (807 Respondents)
I am watching the same number of hours of television this year as I did last year.	59%
The news programs on television are better now than they were five years ago.	70%
The regular network prime-time television programs are better now than they were five years ago.	38%
The overall quality of television is the same now as it was five years ago.	56%
The overall quality of television is worse now than it was five years ago.	37%

10% 20% 30% 40% 50% 60% 70% 80% 90% 100%

1. As you and your partner plan your paragraph, answer the following questions:
   - What does the chart imply about U.S. television viewing habits (probably)?
   - Do you (and your partner) agree with the survey? How are your views similar? How are they different?
   - Why do you (and your partner) think North Americans prefer some kinds of programs and dislike others?

2. As you write, plan your paragraph, and use some of these structures:
   - According to…
   - Most North Americans (XX percent)...
   - Other Americans regularly watch...
   - Some Americans (XX percent) like...
   - In our opinion…

3. As you write your paragraph,
   A. Use comparison and contrast structures.
   B. Use comparative adjectives.
   C. Use appropriate connectors.
   D. Use time words and time clauses.

4. Exchange paragraphs with another pair of classmates. Read their paragraph.

A. (Circle) the comparative adjectives.

B. Put parentheses ( ) around the time clauses. (Circle) the time words for each clause.

C. Underline any errors in the paragraph.

Other Paragraph Topics

- Dinner in My Country vs. Dinner in the United States (or another country)

- How I am similar to

    - a diamond ring?

    - a soccer game?

    - a camel?

    - a detective novel?

    - a pizza?

    - _____

- Teachers in My Country vs. Teachers in the United States (or another country)

- Traffic in My Country vs. Traffic in the United States (or another country)

- My Childhood Beliefs vs. the Reality of Adulthood

Writing Projects

Individual Project: Write several paragraphs about your education in your country. Include paragraphs about some of the following topics:

- The Primary Education System in My Country
    - My Favorite Primary School Memory
    - My Best Primary School Teacher
    - An Adjustment I Made in Primary School
    - An Unforgettable Primary School Experience
    - My Best Friend in Primary School

- The Secondary School System in My Country
  - My Favorite Class (Teacher, Subject) in Secondary School
  - Sports in My Secondary School
  - My Favorite Sport in Secondary School
  - A Terrible Experience in Secondary School
  - My Graduation from Secondary School

Gather these paragraphs into a booklet. Illustrate the booklet with photographs, drawings, and documents from the school(s) you attended. Present the booklet to a local public school for use in their classes.

Group Project: Make a survey about television viewing habits like the one below.

- Ask students NOT in your class to complete the survey.
- Then compile the survey data.
- Summarize the data in chart form and in paragraph form.
- Post the results of the survey on your classroom bulletin board.
- Make copies of the results for the students who participated in the survey.
- Send a copy of the results of the survey to a local television station with some suggestions for changes in programming.

TELEVISION VIEWING SURVEY

Please read the following questions and answer them.

1. Do you watch television? Yes _____   No _____

2. How many hours do you watch each week?
   1–5 _____   7–12 _____   13–20 _____   More than 20 _____

3. What programs do you watch often?
   news programs_____   game shows_____   dramas_____
   movies_____   sports_____   police shows_____
   other (specify)_____

4. Which programs are similar to programs you watch in your country?
   _____

5. Which programs are different from programs you watch in your country?

    _____

6. How are they different?

    _____

7. What are your three favorite programs?

    a. _____

    b. _____

    c. _____

8. What kind of programs do you dislike the most?

    _____

9. Why?

    _____

10. What advice would you give U.S. television producers about U.S. television?

    _____

Appendix A

SOME REGULAR AND IRREGULAR ENGLISH VERBS*

| Root Form | Third Person Singular | PAST | | Special Verbs |
		Regular	Irregular	
admit	admits	admitted		
agree	agrees	agreed		
become	becomes		became	
begin	begins		began	
bite	bites		bit	
blow	blows		blew	
break	breaks		broke	
bring	brings		brought	
build	builds		built	
buy	buys		bought	
catch	catches		caught	
choose	chooses		chose	
come	comes		came	
cost	costs		cost	
cut	cuts		cut	
dance	dances	danced		
dial	dials	dialed		
do	does		did	

SOME REGULAR AND IRREGULAR ENGLISH VERBS* (Continued)

Root Form	Third Person Singular	PAST Regular	Irregular	Special Verbs
draw	draws		drew	
drink	drinks		drank	
drive	drives		drove	
earn	earns	earned		
eat	eats		ate	
end	ends	ended		
enjoy	enjoys	enjoyed		
enter	enters	entered		
excuse	excuses	excused		
fall	falls		fell	
feed	feeds		fed	
feel	feels		felt	
fight	fights		fought	
fill	fills	filled		
find	finds		found	
finish	finishes	finished		
flow	flows	flowed		
fly	flies		flew	
follow	follows	followed		
forget	forgets		forgot	
forgive	forgives		forgave	
get	gets		got	
give	gives		gave	
go	goes		went	
grow	grows		grew	

SOME REGULAR AND IRREGULAR ENGLISH VERBS* (Continued)

Root Form	Third Person Singular	PAST Regular	Irregular	Special Verbs
hang	hangs		hung	
happen	happens	happened		
have	has		had	have to
hear	hears		heard	
help	helps	helped		
hope	hopes	hoped		
hurry	hurries	hurried		
hurt	hurts		hurt	
include	includes	included		
interview	interviews	interviewed		
jump	jumps	jumped		
keep	keeps		kept	
kill	kills	killed		
knock	knocks	knocked		
know	knows		knew	
land	lands	landed		
laugh	laughs	laughed		
learn	learns	learned		
lift	lifts	lifted		
like	likes	liked		
listen	listens	listened		listen to
live	lives	lived		
look	looks	looked		look at
lose	loses		lost	
make	makes		made	

SOME REGULAR AND IRREGULAR ENGLISH VERBS* (Continued)

Root Form	Third Person Singular	PAST Regular	Irregular	Special Verbs
manage	manages	managed		
mean	means		meant	
meet	meets		met	
miss	misses	missed		
move	moves	moved		
need	needs	needed		
offer	offers	offered		
open	opens	opened		
order	orders	ordered		
park	parks	parked		
pay	pays		paid	
pick	picks	picked		
play	plays	played		
prefer	prefers	preferred		
put	puts		put	
rain	rains	rained		
read	reads		read	
remember	remembers	remembered		
request	requests	requested		
return	returns	returned		
ride	rides		rode	
run	runs		ran	
say	says		said	
see	sees		saw	
sell	sells		sold	

SOME REGULAR AND IRREGULAR ENGLISH VERBS* (Continued)

Root Form	Third Person Singular	PAST Regular	Irregular	Special Verbs
send	sends		sent	
serve	serves	served		
shake	shakes		shook	
share	shares	shared		
shine	shines		shone	
sign	signs	signed		
sing	sings		sang	
sit	sits		sat	
sleep	sleeps		slept	
smile	smiles	smiled		
smoke	smokes	smoked		
snow	snows	snowed		
speak	speaks		spoke	
spell	spells	spelled		
spend	spends		spent	
stand	stands		stood	
start	starts	started		
stay	stays	stayed		
stop	stops	stopped		
study	studies	studied		
take	takes		took	
talk	talks	talked		
teach	teaches		taught	
tell	tells		told	
thank	thanks	thanked		

SOME REGULAR AND IRREGULAR ENGLISH VERBS* (Continued)

Root Form	Third Person Singular	PAST Regular	Irregular	Special Verbs
think	thinks		thought	
throw	throws		threw	
travel	travels	travelled		
turn	turns	turned		
type	types	typed		
understand	understands		understood	
use	uses	used		used to
visit	visits	visited		
wait	waits	waited		
wake	wakes		woke	
walk	walks	walked		
want	wants	wanted		
watch	watches	watched		
wear	wears		wore	
win	wins		won	
work	works	worked		
worry	worries	worried		
write	writes		wrote	

*See the spelling rules in Appendix D

Appendix B

SOME ENGLISH ADJECTIVES AND ADVERBS*

Root Form	-er/more than	-est/the most	Adverb
angry	angrier	angriest	angrily
bad	worse**	worst**	badly
beautiful	more beautiful	most beautiful	beautifully
big	bigger	biggest	_____
busy	busier	busiest	busily
careless	more careless	most careless	carelessly
comfortable	more comfortable	most comfortable	comfortably
confusing	more confusing	most confusing	confusingly
convenient	more convenient	most convenient	conveniently
easy	easier	easiest	easily
expensive	more expensive	most expensive	_____
fast	faster	fastest	fast**
frustrating	more frustrating	most frustrating	_____
good	better**	best**	good**
happy	happier	happiest	happily
hard	harder	hardest	hard**
hot	hotter	hottest	_____
important	more important	most important	importantly
intelligent	more intelligent	most intelligent	intelligently
interesting	more interesting	most interesting	interestingly

SOME ENGLISH ADJECTIVES AND ADVERBS*

Root Form	-er/more than	-est/the most	Adverb
large	larger	largest	_____
late	later	latest	_____
lazy	lazier	laziest	lazily
long	longer	longest	_____
noisy	noisier	noisiest	noisily
old	older	oldest	_____
pretty	prettier	prettiest	prettily
quiet	quieter	quietest	quietly
serious	more serious	most serious	seriously
small	smaller	smallest	_____
soft	softer	softest	softly
strong	stronger	strongest	strongly
successful	more successful	most successful	successfully
tall	taller	tallest	_____
terrible	more terrible	most terrible	terribly
useful	more useful	most useful	usefully
warm	warmer	warmest	warmly

*See the spelling rules in Appendix C
**Irregular forms

Appendix C

SPELLING RULES FOR ENGLISH ADJECTIVES

End of Word	Example	-er Ending	-est Ending	Comments
e	white large	whiter larger	whitest largest	Add -**r** or -**st**
2 consonants	dark old	darker older	darkest oldest	Add -**er** or -**est**
1 vowel + 1 consonant	thin big	thinner bigger	thinnest biggest	One-syllable adjective: double final consonant; add -**er** or -**est**
	quiet	quieter	quietest	Two-syllable adjective with stress on first syllable; do not double final consonant.
1 consonant + **y** 2 consonants + **y**	heavy easy pretty	heavier easier prettier	heaviest easiest prettiest	Drop the **y**; add -**ier** or -**iest**

Appendix D

SPELLING RULES FOR ENGLISH VERBS

End of Word	Example	Third Person Singular	-ed Ending	-ing Ending	Comments
-e	smil**e** hop**e**	smil**es** hop**es**	*smil**ed** *hop**ed**	*smil**ing** *hop**ing**	*Drop the final **-e**
2 consonants	wa**lk** lea**rn**	wa**lks** lea**rns**	wa**lked** lea**rned**	wa**lking** lea**rning**	Regular forms
1 vowel + 1 consonant	beg shop	begs shops	**begg**ed** **shop**ped**	**begg**ing** **shop**ping**	**One-syllable verb: double the final consonant
1 vowel + 1 consonant	HAP**pen** VIS**it**	HAPpens VISits	†HAPpen**ed** †VISit**ed**	†HAPpen**ing** †VISit**ing**	†Two-syllable verb with first syllable stressed: do not double the final consonant
1 vowel + 1 consonant	pre**FER** com**MIT**	preFERs comMITs	††preFER**red** ††comMIT**ted**	††preFER**ring** ††comMIT**ting**	††Two-syllable verb with second syllable stressed: double the final consonant

SPELLING RULES FOR ENGLISH VERBS (Continued)

End of Word	Example	Third Person Singular	-ed Ending	-ing Ending	Comments
1 consonant + **-y**	try carry	*tries *carries	*tried *carried	**trying **carrying	*Drop the **-y**; add **-ies** or **-ied** **Do not drop the **-y** for **-ing**
1 vowel + **-y**	stay enjoy	stays enjoys	stayed enjoyed	staying enjoying	Regular forms
-ss -sh **-ch -x**	miss finish watch fix	*misses *finishes *watches *fixes	missed finished watched fixed	missing finishing watching fixing	*Add **-es** to third person singular; then Regular forms

NOTE: Many English verbs have irregular forms.

Examples:	swim	swims	*swam	swimming
	buy	buys	*bought	buying
	catch	catches	*caught	catching

Index